TRAVELLING ALONE

OPTIMA

TRAVELLING ALONE
A GUIDE FOR WORKING WOMEN

ROBERTA BAILEY

ILLUSTRATED BY MAGGIE LING

An OPTIMA book

© Roberta Bailey 1988

First published in 1988 by
Macdonald Optima, a division of
Macdonald & Co. (Publishers) Ltd

A Pergamon Press plc Company

All rights reserved

No part of this publication may be reproduced,
stored in a retrieval system, or transmitted,
in any form or by any means without the prior
permission in writing of the publisher, nor be
otherwise circulated in any form of binding or
cover other than that in which it is published
and without a similar condition including this
condition being imposed on the subsequent
purchaser.

British Library Cataloguing in Publication Data
Bailey, Roberta
    Travelling alone: a guide for working
    women.
    1. Travel — Handbooks, manuals, etc.
    2. Women travellers — Handbooks, manuals, etc.
    I. Title
    910'.2'02   G151

ISBN 0-356-14222-1

Macdonald & Co. (Publishers) Ltd
3rd Floor
Greater London House
Hampstead Road
London NW1 7QX

Typeset by Leaper & Gard, Bristol, England

Printed and bound in Great Britain by
The Guernsey Press Co. Ltd., Guernsey, Channel Islands.

CONTENTS

INTRODUCTION 7

1. FORWARD PLANNING 9
   Choosing the right hotel 9
   Booking in 16
   Moving around 17
   Organizing your appointments 18

2. PREPARING THE PAPERWORK 23
   Documents 23
   Insurance 26
   Money 27

3. THE ART OF PACKING 29
   Choosing a suitcase 29
   How much to take 32
   Hand luggage 41
   Packing tips 42

4. COVERING FOR YOUR ABSENCE 47
   In the office 47
   In the home 49

5. TAKING A POSITIVE APPROACH 53
   Be an assertive traveller 54
   Learning to love your own company 58
   Making the most of your trip 64

6. COPING ALONE 67
   Dealing with unwanted company 67
   Sex and the single traveller 72
   Common sense and self-defence 76

7. TRAVEL AND YOUR HEALTH	85
Sensible health precautions	85
The traveller's first aid kit	92
Medical insurance	93
Travel sickness	95
Avoiding jet lag	97
The stress of travelling and how to minimize it	101
The effects of travel on periods and premenstrual tension	102
8. TRAVELLING MOTHERS	107
Practical pointers	107
Emotional responses	111
9. DIFFERENT COUNTRIES, DIFFERENT CUSTOMS	113
Entertaining	117
10. COMING HOME	121
INDEX	125
ABOUT THE AUTHOR	128

INTRODUCTION

Travel is a wonderful, mind-broadening experience. A friend of mine departs each summer, with less gear than would fall out of my handbag on an average day, to spend a couple of months travelling alone in ever more far-flung places. I love hearing about her experiences when she gets back, as so far she always has done, completely in one piece. This book is definitely not for her, or anyone like her! It is for those of us who would never have dreamed of embarking on a journey all alone, but for whom circumstance has made it happen.

That circumstance is work. Our jobs have given us the opportunity to travel, but have not provided a travelling companion. This book is therefore aimed primarily at the business woman travelling on her own, although much of what is included applies to women travelling alone in any context. This is not to imply that we are all reluctant travellers. We actively want to make those trips, but at the same time admit to some trepidation, at least the first few times, about going alone.

In writing this book, I have talked to a wide variety of women whose experience of travel has been extensive. The advice given throughout the book does not therefore come exclusively from me, but is the product of our combined experience. I hope the sharing of it will help women travelling alone for the first time to recognize the pitfalls, but likewise to identify the enjoyment to be gained. The vast majority of women interviewed travel in a business context, but I was keen to include those intrepid, backpacking souls who, I thought, might ridicule my contention that travelling alone can be difficult or lonely sometimes. They were, in fact, surprisingly sympathetic and admitted to the occasional foundering of their own confidence when things went wrong. What I did gain from them, and what I have tried to bring across, is the sheer

INTRODUCTION

pleasure to be gained from travelling alone. Many women will have to wait a while, and make a lot of journeys, before that solo pleasure becomes heartfelt. One of the aims of this book is to help you reach that point quicker, by making you aware of what to expect, and pointing out ways in which you can make things run more smoothly while away on a trip.

It is hoped that the information in this book will save you from making the mistakes we have made. Much of the advice given may seem obvious when you read it here in black and white. But, believe me, it is not nearly so obvious when you are out there, thinking on your feet — and very tired feet they usually are! Of course, the information cannot be completely comprehensive and you will come across new situations which you will have to tackle. However, the experiences and emotions related should make you aware that you are never the only one who has ever felt like that, that you can and will turn the situation around and that you can and will enjoy the opportunity travel provides.

The book is written specifically for women because it *is* different for us — our biological and emotional differences come into play and we are treated and perceived differently by the people we encounter — so, although much of the advice given in the book could be of equal interest to men, the emphasis is on the way it is for the lone female traveller.

1. FORWARD PLANNING

There are no hard and fast rules on offer here about the best way of travelling alone as a woman, but there is plenty of, hopefully, invaluable advice gleaned from the experiences of women who have travelled extensively, in various parts of the world, in the course of their different jobs. Some of what is said is pure common sense, some of it covers the practicalities involved in travelling generally and much of it is concerned with the specifics of travelling solo as a woman.

One point, in particular, was emphasized by seasoned women travellers — if you are about to travel, on your own, on a business trip, *plan it out carefully in advance*. Obviously you are never going to be able to anticipate every eventuality, too much is unpredictable in the world of travel — and business — but a little forethought and preparation can go a long way to ensuring that you return from a trip feeling that it has been a profitable experience, not only in business terms but also on a more personal level.

CHOOSING THE RIGHT HOTEL

This is the first, and one of the most important tasks for a woman travelling alone. Your choice of hotel is the key to your enjoyment of a business trip — and how much you get out of a trip will undoubtedly affect the success or otherwise of the venture as a whole. So for both personal and work reasons it is worth making some careful investigations into the hotels in the place you are visiting before you book.

FORWARD PLANNING

Be wary about leaving the decision up to a travel agent unless you are able to give him a concise list of your requirements. Provide no more guidance than a vague request such as 'somewhere central' and you might find yourself booked into the red light zone! Likewise, if someone recommends a hotel in the vicinity on the grounds that it is 'quaint and charming', find out exactly what they mean. What counts as 'quaint' during a romantic weekend may well prove positively exasperating when you are trying to keep up with a busy and tiring work schedule.

The following points are worth bearing in mind when trying to choose the right hotel:

1. The best advice on the suitability of a particular hotel will come from someone who has experienced it first-hand

FORWARD PLANNING

— particularly another woman staying alone — so ask around to see if anyone you know has been to that area, or knows someone else who has been. Do not hesitate to telephone the 'friend of a friend of a friend' if she might have first-hand knowledge. There are endless tips that can help ease your passage in unfamiliar territory if the advice comes from someone with direct experience, and even the 'friend eight times removed' will usually be only too keen to pass on her experience to help another business colleague.

The advantage of such advice is that it can reflect the finer nuances of staying alone, such as the 'attitude' of the hotel to women guests, does it make them feel welcome and comfortable or are the staff off-hand and rude, viewing the lone woman as an object of suspicion — an attitude that is unfortunately rather too prevalent among some hotel staff and one that could make your stay unpleasantly uncomfortable.

This said, some hotels, particularly those that are part of the larger chains, are taking positive steps nowadays to ensure that single women feel they are being well catered for, as indeed they should given that women account for a growing proportion of business travellers and are therefore increasingly important as customers. This changing attitude of hotels is reflected in a number of innovations, ranging from the small but welcome detail of hairdryers in all bathrooms to setting aside entire floors for female guests only. This latter idea has grown out of the enthusiasm that customers showed for being given the choice of smoking or non-smoking rooms, or even the non-smoking floors some hotels are now offering. If either of these ideas appeals to you, enquire directly with the hotel or ask your travel agent if they know of any hotels offering these options.

2. If a recommendation for a particular hotel is being given by people who had stayed in it while on holiday, consider what they say carefully and bear in mind that what might be ideal for a couple on holiday will not

FORWARD PLANNING

necessarily be so for the lone business woman. Ask them to expand on particular points so you can assess whether or not the hotel would meet your specific requirements. For instance, it might be perfect for a holiday to opt for a hotel 'at the centre of the local nightlife', but do you really want to lie awake at night after a busy day of meetings eavesdropping on the conversation of the diners enjoying an alfresco meal below your bedroom window, or listening to the throb of the local disco?

Be sure to ask what the hotel rooms are like. If you are travelling on business you are likely to spend more time in your room than you would perhaps if you were there on holiday or attending a conference with other colleagues. If the description then proffered suggests the rooms are pokey and claustrophobic, or are poorly sound-proofed, think again. Such conditions may be tolerable if you are enjoying yourself on the beach all day and out wining and dining all night, but they are not conducive to winding down and relaxing at the end of a hard day of business negotiations.

3. If you are not sure about hotels in a particular locality and cannot find anyone who has been there themselves, think about opting for a hotel which comes under the umbrella of one of the major hotel chains, such as the Holiday Inns. Many women who travel regularly recommend this course of action. Although it might mean forfeiting 'character and charm', you are at least guaranteed that the hotel will conform to a particular standard wherever it may be in the world, and that it will provide decent-sized, sound-proofed rooms, efficient room service, telex facilities, a dry cleaning service for clothes and all the other facilities which business people need. Another advantage is that such hotels usually provide a wide range of places to eat, giving you the opportunity to choose between a snack in your room, a light meal in the café or a four-course gourmet's delight in the main dining room.

FORWARD PLANNING

Je t'adore

4. Unless you abolutely loathe television, make sure you pick a hotel that can offer television in every room. A TV set can be surprisingly companionable when you are a long way from home, even if it is just burbling away in the background as you take your shower, or talking to you in a language you do not understand. If you do understand the language, then television can provide a welcome source of easy entertainment if you find yourself facing a few hours alone. Another bonus is that television programmes, including the advertisements, can afford many social and cultural insights into the country in which you are staying, and provide information on some of the pertinent national events of the moment, all of which will serve you well when dealing with the people you have come to meet for business.

5. As one business woman pointed out, the ritziest, most glamorous hotels are often best avoided. As a merchant banker, she could stay in some of the most expensive hotels, but said that she now gives the smartest hotel in town a miss and selects instead a comfortable, medium-category hotel with a full range of facilities. The reason? The smaller hotels are nearly always friendly and welcoming, she says, far more so than their flashier

FORWARD PLANNING

counterparts, and that helps her to feel at ease and settle in so she can get on with her job effectively.

Besides trying to find the right 'type' of hotel, you have to look at a number of other practical factors before deciding on a hotel.

Location
One of these practical points is the hotel's location — is it situated in a convenient part of the town or city in terms of your business requirements? It will save you time, and your company money, if you stay in a hotel near to where the majority of your appointments are located. This is also well worth organizing from the point of view of personal comfort and convenience, as it will mean you can get back to your hotel in those awkward half-hours that can crop up between meetings, despite your best attempts at planning. If you are encumbered by heavy samples or even a weighty briefcase, anything else you could do to fill those gaps — shopping or sightseeing for instance — is no fun at all!

Oddly enough, though, staying too close to your appointments can be a distinct drawback if you have heavy loads to carry — taxi drivers loathe just driving you round the corner. In fact they will often refuse to do so. If your encumbrances make it impossible for you to walk to your appointments, you would be better served by staying just far enough away to justify a taxi ride. So whenever you end up staying too far or too near on any particular trip, make a point of looking out for some more suitably placed accommodation for next time.

Facilities offered
Be sure to check out in advance exactly what facilities a hotel can offer you. Enquire, for instance, about whether the hotel provides dinner as well as breakfast. Unless you are dining with clients you probably will not want to walk round unfamiliar streets alone at night searching for a suitable restaurant. It is also worth asking if they provide

FORWARD PLANNING

snacks or light meals as well as four-course dinners — your appetite may not be up to a gourmet delight every night.

Ask, too, about the rooms; how large are they, how well-appointed, and so on. As a lone traveller you are quite likely to spend a fair amount of your 'off-duty' time in your room and you need to be assured that it will provide a relaxing and comfortable environment in which you can unwind after a hectic day. A great aid to unwinding is a long hot bath and for a woman travelling alone a private en suite bathroom should always be viewed as a necessity, never a luxury. So always make sure your room has a private bathroom.

It is well worth trying to find a hotel which offers a swimming pool, sauna and/or gym facilities. Many of the hotels in the main chains do offer such facilities and they can provide you with a pleasant way of exercising and relaxing after work, rather than just flopping on your bed with a book.

Parking

If you are travelling by car, don't underestimate the importance of booking a hotel which has garage or parking facilities. Whilst this is absolutely standard in many locations — driving through the USA, for example, parking is never a problem when you pull off the freeway into one of the myriad of hotels, motels and motor lodges that make travel so convenient — hotels in big cities everywhere in the world have problems in offering their clients somewhere to park. In this respect, the modern 'chain' hotels once again score over older, characterful hotels, many of which date back to an era when horsepower meant just that.

Being able to park at your hotel means convenience — not having to drag your luggage from several blocks away, not getting wet if it rains, and so on. It also means safety — not having to search for parking space in unfamiliar locations and not having to walk back to your hotel alone at night. Remember, however, that garage parking does

15

FORWARD PLANNING

not guarantee the safety of your car. Thefts from cars parked in hotel car parks are unfortunately rather common, so take all your valuable belongings into the hotel with you. If you have an estate car, which means that your luggage is visible, you would be wise to take all your belongings into the hotel. For ease, keep what you need for an overnight stay in a separate smaller bag, so that you do not have to open up your entire luggage.

If you are driving abroad, hotel parking has the added bonus of avoiding the necessity of understanding the parking restrictions and penalties of the country in which you are travelling. These can often be exasperatingly arcane. It can be very stressful to be driving around searching for that elusive parking space as you watch the time of your appointment come — and go. Or even worse, to return wearily to your car to find it has been towed away or clamped for infringing parking regulations you did not know even existed.

BOOKING IN

When you check in at your hotel, ask for a room on the quiet side of the hotel (assuming it has one!). If you have any problem sleeping in noisy surroundings, a view of the rubbish bins at the back of the hotel will serve you very much better than the view of the street with its jolly pavement cafes. Look around carefully at your room when you are taken to it, because if there is anything you do not like, this is the time to ask for a different room. Before you start to unpack, try out the plumbing — do all the taps work, is the water hot enough? Are there any extraneous noises which will disturb you — a dripping tap, a whirring air-conditioning unit, a generator right outside your window? Is the TV/radio/minibar working? If you are not completely satifisfied, never be shy to complain and ask for a change of room if necessary. Minor annoyances can prevent your settling in quickly and sleeping properly, both of which are important to your frame of mind during your stay.

FORWARD PLANNING

Some noise is inevitable in hotels; they are 'public places' after all, and you must expect occasional noise from room to room, or from the corridor. However, you do not have to put up with excessive noise. If someone is throwing a noisy party or playing music or their TV far too loud, don't suffer in silence as this will only make you tense and irritable. Instead of trying to deal with the problem directly yourself, telephone down to the reception desk and ask them to make contact with the offending guest. Most hotels act promptly on this — you are probably not the only person being disturbed — and most guests readily comply, possibly not having realized the nuisance they were causing.

Occasionally, of course, you will come up against behaviour that is purely antisocial and will have little option but to grit your teeth and bear it. In these cases a mild sleeping tablet is a good alternative to lying awake half the night and feeling wretched the following day.

MOVING AROUND

When you are travelling and finding hotels as you move on rather than booking in advance, take care to arrive at your

FORWARD PLANNING

next venue at a time of day which will give you the best chance of getting accommodation. Check-out time is normally around midday and it is only then that hotels can be sure how many empty rooms they have for that night. If you arrive shortly after midday, you will have the best possible chance of obtaining one of those rooms and will also be able to occupy it straight away. It is quite acceptable, and very sensible, to ask to take a look at the room before you agree to take it, although you may not be able to afford the luxury of turning it down if accommodation has proved hard to find.

If you are travelling without prior reservations, be sure to take with you a good guide book which lists hotels and gives a description of them in terms of category and facilities. It can save an enormous amount of time if you have already singled out two or three to try in order of preference. Alternatively, the local tourist office may be able to help you to find suitable accommodation. If this draws a blank, there are always the room touts as a last resort. They usually work from the railway stations, docks or airports and can offer a room in a private house or a small pension which will normally be clean and perfectly acceptable — certainly a million times better than having nowhere to stay at all.

ORGANIZING YOUR APPOINTMENTS

The client comes first

Before making your travel plans, check that your key clients will actually be there and can see you at the time you hope to make your trip. Many business trips start off on the wrong foot because people tend to make their travel plans first — a certain week works well for them in terms of their own personal and work schedule and so reservations are made. Only then do they start to make appointments and discover that one or two key people are too busy to see them then, or are away on holiday. So, the advice is always to check out your most important appointments first, before any other plans are made.

National holidays
You will also need to check on holiday periods for the country you are visiting. Some countries have national 'shut-down' periods; for example, much of Scandinavia is 'closed' during July, whilst France goes on holiday in August. Depending on the nature of your business, your clients may or may not follow the established pattern, but check this out to be sure. Tourist offices or embassies can provide information as to when national holidays fall and you can ask other people who travel to that country, or indeed your business contacts who are usually only too pleased to advise you when to visit — if only to prevent you turning up at unsuitable times!

Remember that it is always worth ensuring that a visit is not too close to the start or finish of a holiday period, as these always tend to be busy periods and your client will probably be most reluctant to receive visitors in the midst of it. Equally important, it could undermine the effectiveness of your visit if it is made just before a holiday, as any follow up will be delayed and the impact of your visit may be diminished if your contact is not in a position to take any action until his or her return.

It is also worth bearing in mind that public holidays, whilst they may only officially affect one day of your proposed visit, can actually cut further into it. Many people take additional days either side of a public holiday, so check that you will not in fact be losing a further day's business, either in the week containing the holiday or the previous/following week.

Finally, check on business hours in the country concerned. This will enable you to know how early in the day you can start making appointments and how late you can work.

Planning a schedule

You may find the following suggestions useful when you come to put together a schedule of appointments:

1. Equip yourself with a street map. Once again, tourist offices or embassies can usually provide these (always bring one back from your trip for next time, particularly if you have obtained a clearer map locally). This will enable you to try to group your appointments according to their mutual proximity and cut down on time spent getting from one to another — always a problem on a hectic visit.

2. Decide at the outset which contacts you want to invite to lunch or dinner, or who is likely to suggest this to you. Start by organizing these 'anchor' appointments and work outwards on either side. In this way, you will also avoid asking for appointments with people you do not know so well around the pre-lunch period, which may embarrass them into feeling they are obliged to offer you lunch.

3. Be realistic — rather than simply optimistic — about the time required for each appointment or you might find

FORWARD PLANNING

yourself on a nightmare schedule which allows very little time for getting from one place to another, and no time at all to overrun on an appointment. If it does work out this way, despite your efforts to plan, you must be in full control of your meetings. Like all good stories, each meeting should have a beginning, a middle and an end. Don't let yourself be distracted or diverted from the purpose of your visit.

4. If you plan to visit clients for the first time, it is well worth sending on ahead of your visit some details (brochures, maybe samples) of what you intend to discuss, or what you will be trying to sell them or wish to buy from them. This gives them the opportunity to become familiar with your company and its products before you arrive, allowing them to prepare their queries and requests. This will undoubtedly save you time when you arrive in giving background information and will help make your meeting more effective, more productive — more 'targeted', to use an overworked, but apt expression. Occasionally a client may come back to you to cancel your meeting after receiving advance information and realizing you have no common ground. This prevents a time-wasting appointment and allows you to slot in someone else, or take time for market research.

Market research

Research is something you should try to find time for in between appointments, whether it be looking at the competition for your products or service, or acquiring relevant literature — trade publications, statistical information — which could be important to your strategy for that market.

So when planning a schedule for a trip, leave some time for doing market research in each of the areas. Each time you visit an area or country for which you have responsibility, try to increase your knowledge of the economic, political and social factors affecting it. This will

FORWARD PLANNING

Could you tell me what percentage of left-wing working-class women use sun tan oil?

help you direct your own efforts more profitably, by showing which areas to concentrate on according to the 'climate' affecting your particular business. Do not lose the opportunity to ask questions of the people you are visiting which go beyond the narrow context of your common business interests. You can build up as effective a picture of the place in this way as you can from local newspapers and television.

2.
PREPARING THE PAPERWORK

There are a number of essentials to attend to before travelling abroad, whether your trip is for a few days or a few weeks. First you need to check that you have all the documents you will require for the trip, that you have sufficient funds to see you through and that are you are adequately insured in case anything should go wrong. Once these are all organized, you can try your hand at that most exasperating of tasks — packing!

DOCUMENTS

Top of the list of essential documents is, of course, your *passport*. Is it still valid? Is it a full 10-year British passport? A British visitor's passport cannot be used for *paid* business travel abroad. Bear in mind that it can take a month or more for a new passport to come through the system, unless you are able to go to a passport office in person and even then you will need to set aside most of a day to get a new passport organized. If you travel a lot it might be worth getting the 94-page version so that it does not fill up too quickly with stamps and visas.

Note: Take a note of your passport number and the place and date of issue and keep it separate from your passport. This information will speed up the process of supplying a new passport should yours be lost or stolen while you are away.

When you book your trip with a travel agent or airline ask whether or not you need a *visa* for the country or countries

PREPARING THE PAPERWORK

you plan to visit. Countries that do require visas include the United States of America, Australia, Hungary, Romania, most countries in the Middle East and some in Africa. If you do need a visa, you must apply to the embassy or consulate of the country concerned, supplying passport-type photographs with your application and sometimes a letter from your employer stating that you are visiting the country on business and will be returning home once the business is completed. Most countries also charge a fee for the visa.

Should your trip be to more than one country that requires a visa, your passport will have to be sent to each embassy in turn for stamping. This can take several weeks, so leave plenty of time.

Some countries have *special requirements* and if you are at all unsure, consult the relevant embassy or consulate before setting off. Saudi Arabia, for instance, will only permit you to enter on business and you will need to carry an appropriate letter from your employer with you; the USSR will only welcome you as part of an organized group unless special arrangements are made for your visit; and most Arab countries will not permit entry if your passport is stamped showing that you have visited Israel. If you do need to travel from Israel to an Arab country you will have to arrange for two passports, so you can have a separate one for your Israeli trip. If the Israeli stamp is from a previous trip, you will have to surrender your old passport and apply for a new one.

Other documents to carry with you include:

Tickets — always check your tickets as soon as you receive them, and that the dates and times are as you requested;
Insurance documents — always check that you are adequately insured when travelling abroad (see below);
Proof of identification — keep this separate from your passport;
Driving licence — you never know when you might want to hire a car and it doubles as an alternative proof of

PREPARING THE PAPERWORK

identification. Check with the travel agent or with one of the motoring organizations if you will need an *international drivers' licence* for your destination; *Receipts* — for items such as watches and cameras that are new, otherwise you may be challenged on your return at customs and have to prove that you did not buy the items abroad.

If you are given documents in the course of your travels, keep them until you are *sure* you no longer need them, even if you do not know precisely their function, which can often be the case when language barriers do not allow you to ask. One business woman recounted how in Darjeeling she had thrown away some documents she had needed when entering India. Travelling overland to Nepal, she was asked for what she soon realized were those same documents on exiting the country. She was obliged to travel back to her hotel in Darjeeling and had the great good fortune to find the documents in the hotel's rubbish heap. However the experience was not very pleasant *and* she lost two days out of her trip. She now recommends, 'Keep *every* piece of paper you are given until you get home!'

PREPARING THE PAPERWORK

Failure to have documents stamped in the right places can also result in delays. I have known colleagues travelling on business with goods requiring customs documents who have been sent back to the last border because a stamp had not been obtained. The rules and regulations can seem unfathomable and my advice is to show all documents you have been given to *any* official who stops you — even via sign language, you should be able to work out what you have to do.

INSURANCE

Unfortunately a great many things can go wrong on a trip which is why it is important to take out suitable insurance. The main risks you need cover for are:

medical expenses (see chapter 7)
damage to or loss of your luggage
loss of money
personal accident causing disability or death
personal liability

Some policies also offer cover for flight delays or if you miss a flight. If you are travelling abroad often it might be worth taking out an annual insurance policy — this offers 12 months' protection however many trips you make in that year.

One important point — check that the limits set by the insurance company on the amount you can claim in each section are sufficient. For instance, if you are carrying expensive samples to show a client, you might find that the cover for loss of or damage to luggage is not enough and you will need to negotiate extra cover for this risk. Remember too, that as you are travelling on business, you are likely to have with you some of your smarter clothes. It can cost a fortune to replace such items should your luggage go astray or get stolen if you do not have sufficient insurance to cover the loss. Even if your company arranges insurance for you, ask exactly what cover is offered and top it up with a policy of your own if

PREPARING THE PAPERWORK

you do not feel the cover is adequate. Insurance companies, banks, motoring organizations and travel operators all provide good travel insurance.

As well as the financial limits for claims check the exclusion clauses in an insurance policy, particularly those relating to illness and injury (see chapter 7), and be sure to read the paragraph on 'How to make a claim'. You will find that many claims have a time limit attached e.g. 'Notice has to be given within *24 hours* to the police of any loss or theft or to the carriers when loss or damage occurs in transit', and failure to comply can jeopardize your claim.

MONEY

Work out carefully how much money you will need while you are away. Consider how much you are likely to spend per day on incidental items and add some extra for emergencies which might include a few extra days away for reasons such as transportation delays, illness, business demands.

Now decide how to take the money. It is only common sense not to carry large amounts of cash with you, but you should have enough in *each of the currencies* you will need on your trip to cover transportation from your point of arrival to your hotel, plus a small float to cover emergencies; if you are delayed for any reason, the bureau de change at the airport or station may have closed.

Note: if you do have to carry valuables with you, put them in a money belt, not a handbag which can be snatched, and ask for them to be kept in the hotel's safe once you have arrived there rather than carrying them around with you.

Besides cash you can have access to funds via:

Travellers' cheques — these can be in sterling or in a foreign currency. Your travel agent or airline will be able to tell you which currency is most easily negotiated in the

PREPARING THE PAPERWORK

country to which you are travelling. For instance, it may pay you to take travellers' cheques in US dollars or Japanese yen rather than in sterling. Also remember to shop around when you come to cashing in your travellers' cheques; exchange rates vary, with hotels usually offering the worst deal.

If your travellers' cheques are lost or stolen while you are away, they can usually be replaced. Check that the issuing bank has offices in the country you are visiting so that any loss can be dealt with quickly and a cash advance arranged if you have been left penniless.

Note: sign each cheque as soon as you get them and keep a note of the serial numbers separately in case you need to replace them because of loss or theft.

Credit cards (Access and Visa) and charge cards (American Express and Diners' Club) — these are invaluable as a back-up to travellers' cheques and cash. 'Plastic money' has become universal currency, but check which cards are most commonly accepted in the country you are visiting — the travel agent or relevant embassy or tourist office will be able to advise you. Often a combination of cards is your best bet.

Note: be sure to keep a separate note of the numbers of each of the credit cards you take with you, together with the appropriate telephone numbers so you can report any loss as quickly as possible.

Eurocheques — holding a bank account in an EEC member country entitles you to Eurocheques which can be used throughout Europe. These are supplied with a special Eurocheque guarantee card. Eurocheques are written in local currency, so saving the commission normally charged on changing travellers' cheques, unless, of course, you have had travellers' cheques issued in the currency of the country which you are visiting.

3.
THE ART OF PACKING

Most people approach packing with at least a little trepidation — all those soul-searching decisions about what to take and what to leave behind, wondering how to prepare for every eventuality while still being able to lift the suitcase off the floor! Before you think about what to pack, however, you have to give some thought to what you are going to pack it all in.

CHOOSING A SUITCASE

One golden rule is never trust a fine, elegant suitcase to the care of an airline. By the time your case has been

29

THE ART OF PACKING

thrown around by baggage handlers, bumped and banged on uncaring conveyor belts and squashed beneath goodness knows how many other cases in the hold of an aircraft, the chances of it being returned to you in any of its original glory are remote indeed.

Opt instead for a solid functional suitcase, one that is robust, has a rigid frame, reinforced corners and is made of a durable material which will stand up to rough treatment. If possible, choose one that has wheels — if you are trying to cope with heavy or bulky luggage, wheels can make all the difference and stop your blood pressure reaching dangerous levels. The suitcases which have retractable wheels are the best sort. If the wheels do not retract when not in use they are in danger of getting knocked off by the rough treatment already described, and attachable wheels display an exasperating tendency to slip or fall off at crucial moments.

If you prefer a suitcase which is a little more lightweight, those made of plastic or waterproof nylon are a better choice than the ones made of canvas, which become alarmingly sodden if exposed to any rain on their

THE ART OF PACKING

journey to and from the hold of the plane. Of the foldaway nylon variety, experience has shown that the barrel-shaped type stand up the best to rough handling. However remember that such lightweight suitcases offer little protection for delicate items and are not at all good at keeping clothes in an uncreased condition, so whenever possible it is wisest to choose a case that is as light as possible but which does not sacrifice the qualities of rigidity and robustness. This is equally true whatever your means of transport.

If you are travelling by air and your trip is a relatively short one — or you are an expert in the art of minimal packing — consider using a carry-on bag only. Most luggage manufacturers now offer cases which are functional in terms of space but which still meet the size requirements set out by the airlines for cabin luggage. This can save you a considerable amount of valuable time — not to mention aggravation — when you arrive at the airport of your destination.

Whatever suitcase you choose it should be capable of being locked. The lightweight varieties do not usually have integral locks so you will need to lock the zip with a small padlock. Obviously this will not stop the determined thief but it may just deter the petty pilferer. Whilst on the subject of security, do not write your home address on the label tied to the handle of your suitcase. A recent study into why so many houses were burgled while the owners were away on holiday, as opposed to just out for the day at work, revealed that thieves would select a house to burgle by wandering around at airports, railway stations or ports reading the addresses on the baggage labels of the travellers waiting to depart!

If you have a business address you could use this on your labels, or you can buy labels where you write the address on the inside and then click them shut. Alternatively you could write your home address on the inside of the case, say on the inside of the lid, and just put the address of your destination on the label on the outside.

THE ART OF PACKING

HOW MUCH TO TAKE

Packing for your business requirements
Travelling on business, you will often have less control over the amount you have to carry than when you travel for pleasure — when you really only have yourself to blame if you have packed too much. Presentation kits, samples, artwork, documents, etc, may be essential to your business, and they can mount up to an enormous weight of baggage before you have even started on your personal belongings.

There is one point on which the majority of experienced women travellers are in complete unison — unless you absolutely cannot avoid it, do not travel alone with more than you can carry by yourself, if only for a few paces at a time. If you do so, you will be vulnerable and unable to manage if no help is at hand. The situation could easily arise where you would have to carry your baggage forward bit by bit, with the result that the cases you have to leave unattended are stolen. You also become prey to offers of help from unscrupulous people, which are hard to refuse when it is patently obvious that you cannot manage alone.

THE ART OF PACKING

Here are some hints for reducing your load:

1. If you are undertaking your trip in a sales capacity, take a good hard look at what you intend to take with you. Are some of the items really necessary? Can they be condensed, or taken in a different form? For instance, can a photograph substitute for the real thing in some cases? Is the display method chosen forcing you to take an outsize artwork bag or portfolio, whereas some adjustments would allow a smaller bag to be used? Why not take this opportunity to create some more readily portable sales material?

2. Consider carefully if there are any materials — samples, brochures, etc — which you could send on ahead. Obviously there are some items you will have to carry with you, but sending materials out in advance not only reduces the load for you but also gives your client time to examine them before your meeting.

3. Travelling in a 'buying' capacity can also have its drawbacks. You will invariably come back more laden down than when you went, having acquired samples en route, so you would be well advised to take an extra, relatively empty, suitcase or bag. Buying one locally may prove difficult in terms of time and finding the right type of case and, depending on where you are, could also prove very expensive.

Unless you need to have samples quickly, or are worried that they may not arrive, ask for them to be sent to you. This will also avoid the possibility of your being challenged by customs on your return — they have a habit of wanting to take a look at large quantities of baggage!

Whilst on the subject of customs, if you are unsure whether you need to declare a particular item you are carrying, or whether you need any accompanying documentation, always check beforehand, as this will save you a lot of time and trouble if it turns out you did! You can ask the customs authorities themselves, or you can seek advice from courier or freight companies. They have to keep themselves up-to-date on the current regulations applying in different countries.

THE ART OF PACKING

Choosing clothes

For travelling   The emphasis should always be on comfort when choosing an outfit for a journey. Fortunately these days that does not necessarily mean you have to sacrifice style. Comfortable clothes are particularly important on long journeys when you may need to contort your body into a position in which you can sleep, or try to. Trousers are very practical, although tight ones should be avoided, particularly if you are susceptible to cystitis or thrush. Track suits are the preference of many for travelling, especially as most stores nowadays offer a wide selection of track suits, ranging from sporty to dressy.

Travel clothes should be loose-fitting and made of comfortable, natural fibres. It is wise to avoid light colours, or worse still, white, as you can almost guarantee that the trip will make your clothes grubby. Darker clothes will disguise this better. Avoid one-piece outfits with trousers — you will find it almost impossible to manoeuvre in the confined space of the toilet on most forms of transport, but especially aircraft. Do not trust any garment with a troublesome zip — it is just waiting for the most embarrassing moment to break! It is, in any case, a good idea to wear longish garments on top, which cover skirt or trouser zips and would therefore conceal a broken one. A few safety pins carried as a matter of course will help you deal with this and other disasters, such as missing buttons in crucial places!

If you are travelling at the end of a business day, so want to change before the journey, keep a change of clothes near the top of your suitcase or in a separate bag and change at the airport/port/station. There are often facilities at all of these for you to take a shower, which is highly recommended to refresh you for the journey ahead.

Bear in mind that during the journey it will either be hotter or colder than when you start out, seldom the same, so your choice of clothes should allow for changes in temperature — a jacket or sweater that can be removed if

THE ART OF PACKING

it is hot and stuffy and put on if it turns chilly, for example. Aircraft can be particularly cold whilst airborne, even though they may seem extremely stuffy when you embark, and your body temperature can easily drop. Most aeroplanes carry blankets and on long-haul flights one is usually allocated to every seat. On shorter flights, the supply of blankets can be limited, so it is worth asking the stewardess for one early on or you could easily miss out. Use the blanket in preference to your coat or jacket, which will travel better in an overhead locker rather than crumpled around your body!

Clothes to take with you   Let's look first at the practical side of what you should take. The first step is to find out what the climate is like in the country or countries where you will be travelling and choose clothes accordingly. Then assume anything can happen and probably will, so take at least one outfit which will save you if it turns unexpectedly cold, hot or wet. The skill lies in paring down your personal belongings without leaving out the essentials.

Don't overlook your extremities! It is very easy to forget, as you pack warm clothes when the weather at home is hot, that you will also need gloves, scarves, and headgear if you are travelling to a cold climate. A hat is particularly important in a really cold environment, as a large proportion of the body's heat is lost through the top of the head. Suitable footwear — with an emphasis on the suitable — is another vital consideration. If you know that there will be ice and snow on the ground, take footwear with ridged rubber soles to give you a good grip. Don't assume you will manage in your much smarter leather-soled boots with four-inch heels, even if you are going for a very short time — it takes only seconds to slip and injure yourself!

Likewise, if the weather will be hot (and particularly if it will be humid), pay attention to your feet and leave shoes made from man-made materials at home in favour of soft, loose leather or canvas. Cotton is the best material

THE ART OF PACKING

for hot countries, as it is very effective at absorbing sweat! Clothes should be loose-fitting, light-weight and light-coloured to reflect the heat. Also, if you are sensitive to the sun take a hat and, of course, sunglasses.

Whatever the weather, always take with you a pair of shoes that are particularly comfortable. Then, if the worst comes to the worst and your feet swell up or blister badly, you will still be able to walk. They may not be as elegant as you would wish for a business meeting, but at least they will get you there.

Always take 'back up' clothing. To demonstrate, I offer you some of the pitfalls of travelling *too* light:

I once had the clever — I thought — idea of taking one dark skirt and a selection of blouses for a trip lasting two or three days, but my zip broke on the first day. Having to buy another skirt caused havoc with my schedule and was expensive as I didn't have time to shop around.

Clothes can play dirty tricks on you, for instance, they can crease alarmingly, have a tendency to swivel round or ride up, or do totally unexpected things. A wool suit of mine once got wet in a downpour. Travelling up in the lift with

THE ART OF PACKING

my business acquaintance, I looked round to see if someone had an old dog with them. To my horror I realized it was my suit! The combination of wet wool and, presumably, dry-cleaning fluid was exuding the most awful smell. Luckily, I had already learnt my lesson about having back-up clothes so had other outfits with me and was able to have the suit cleaned after a rather embarrassing afternoon of meetings.

Useful hints mentioned time and time again by women experienced in the art of selecting clothes for a business trip include:

1. Take only tried and tested clothes with you, those in which you feel comfortable, whose habits you know and which you are sure will last an entire day looking relatively pristine. Clothes which crease badly will make you feel self-conscious and uncomfortable

2. Don't take those smart outfits hanging in your wardrobe which you feel you *ought* to wear — after all, you paid a lot of money for them — but which you know do not suit you despite their expense. You are no more

THE ART OF PACKING

likely to wear them on your trip and they will just take up space and add dead weight to your suitcase.

3. Choose your fabrics carefully for their crease-resistant powers. Good fabrics are cotton or wool mixtures with synthetic fibres, but, for comfort, the greater proportion in the mix should be the natural fibre. Remember that you will need pure cotton garments if you are going somewhere very hot and, similarly, pure wool garments if the climate will be very cold. Notoriously bad fabrics are linen and silk, so avoid these if you can. You will soon get to know which clothes just hang out all their creases overnight and start to rely on these.

Note: It is vital, however tired you are when you arrive, to hang up your clothes straight away. A good tip for dealing with creases which are a little more stubborn, or when you need to uncrease an outfit in a hurry, is to hang the garment in the bathroom and turn on the hot water to make the room steamy. Steam can do wonders for creases. However, make sure the garment is absolutely dry again before you wear it! Needless to say, a travel iron is a great boon.

THE ART OF PACKING

4. Make a checklist of items of clothing you want to take, just to ensure that nothing is left out. Most forgotten articles of clothing are panties and petticoats! It is so easy to be concentrating on your outward appearance when selecting your clothes that you completely forget about your underwear. Petticoats are especially easy to forget if you are setting forth in a lined skirt or trousers.

5. If you are seeing different people every day on a business trip, it is not necessary to have a different outfit for each day of your trip — only *you* will know that you have worn that dress the day before, your clients will not.

What your clothes say about you

What you wear when travelling has more significance than mere practicality; you need to be aware of the fact that what you wear can say a great deal about you. Certainly, when travelling on business, you can easily be judged at face value by the way you present yourself. You might increase your 'foreignness' by dressing too flamboyantly and most female travellers tend to favour dressing to blend in with their surroundings as a method of integration — and a way of avoiding unwanted attention. Time and time again, women have told me that they take 'subdued' clothes with them on lone trips, nothing too colourful, nothing too low-cut.

It is important always to respect any particular code of dress which applies in the countries you are visiting. It would be foolish to go around with bare arms in many Arab countries, for example; your hosts would be insulted and you risk being pestered continually. Whatever your feelings are about the sense or otherwise of the rule concerned, cover up as appropriate and you will find your progress much easier than if you opt for defiance. It is a mark of respect for your hosts to observe their standards of dress and avoid giving offence by wearing shorts when visiting a temple or going into a church with bare head and shoulders. Look around at what local women wear, particularly in Islamic countries, and cover up as much as

THE ART OF PACKING

is practicable, given the climate and the clothes you have available.

One business woman who has travelled alone extensively in India recounted how she used to find her steps dogged by people poking and pulling at her clothes. Much as she was assured that this was a sign of polite interest, she found it irritating and actually spoiling her enjoyment of her surroundings; if she stopped to look at something interesting, the prying fingers would multiply. She decided to change to Indian style garments at one point on her journey and, lo and behold, the pestering stopped.

The question of dressing in local clothes is one on which opinions are sharply divided; many women feel that local clothes have evolved like that because they are the most practical and comfortable for the climate and therefore it makes good sense to adopt them. Others feels that this is a

THE ART OF PACKING

condescending approach, or that it would be like putting on fancy dress. Whether you adopt local styles or not, dressing in an appropriate way in terms of covering up where necessary is strongly advised — both you and your hosts will feel more comfortable.

HAND LUGGAGE

The scenario where you travel East and your luggage travels West is a well-known one to the experienced traveller. If this happens to you, take heart — lost luggage generally reappears, although it may take several days to do so. For this reason it is wise to consider carefully what to pack in your hand luggage — it may be all you have to survive with for a while!

Airlines do offer passengers whose luggage has gone astray an 'overnight kit'. Unfortunately these seem to be geared towards the male rather than the female traveller. Hopefully some airline will come up with a kit designed to meet a woman's needs before too long, but in the meantime the advice from seasoned women travellers is always to pack your own 'survival kit' and keep it with you on the plane as hand luggage.

The overnight kit should contain as a minimum:

Toothbrush and toothpaste
Deodorant
Soap and shampoo
Hairbrush and/or comb
Hairdryer
Make-up
Nightdress
Change of underwear
Spare pair of tights
Any medicines you need regularly, eg the Pill
Sanitary towels or tampons

You should always pack in your hand luggage anything valuable or irreplaceable, just in case your luggage disappears permanently. It can be heartbreaking, for

THE ART OF PACKING

instance, to lose a favourite piece of jewellery because of an airline's mistake, so never trust such items to luggage you are going to check-in.

Note: If your luggage does not appear on the baggage carousel at the airport of your destination, report that it is missing to the airline concerned immediately. Then ask them what compensation you can expect for the time you will be deprived of your belongings, drawing their attention to the fact that you have a very important meeting first thing tomorrow morning for which you will now have to purchase a new set of clothes. Airlines are empowered to offer you amounts of money, determined by the length of time your luggage remains missing — a service that most airlines are reluctant to advertise. You are entitled to this compensation if their error is causing you inconvenience, so persist until an amount has been agreed upon and they have told you how they will pay you.

PACKING TIPS

Obviously what you choose to take with you depends on personal preference, the length of your trip and where you are going. However you will probably find that there are a number of items which you nearly always want to take with you and which you would miss should you forget to pack any of them. For this reason it is a good idea to make a checklist of essential items which you can keep in your suitcase ready for reference every time you come to do your packing for a business trip.

I canvassed a number of women who are experienced travellers about what items they would include on such a checklist, and from their answers I have been able to compile the top twenty items. These are not listed in any particular order of merit, but were the items that were mentioned most often as essential for a trip. The list may help when you come to think of making your own checklist.

THE ART OF PACKING

Personal stereo, plus favourite tapes
Travel alarm clock
Hairdryer
Travel iron
Travel adaptor
Earplugs
Sewing kit
Umbrella (doubles as sunshade)
Washing powder/cream
Torch
Camera
Travel kettle/element, plus teabags or sachets of coffee and powdered milk
Bathplug (a must for travellers to the USSR or Eastern Europe — hotels there rarely supply them)
Calculator
Business cards
Safety pins (for dealing with missing buttons in crucial places)
A pillow (if you have room in your luggage and if you find it difficult to sleep on unfamiliar pillows or are allergic to feathers, for instance)
A selection of good books
Knitting, embroidery or whatever pastime is transportable and relaxing

THE ART OF PACKING

Writing paper and envelopes (writing home can be very therapeutic)

One of the biggest headaches with packing is how to get everything you need (or think you need) into the amount of space available. One answer is to make items as small as possible. Go through your cosmetics, for instance, and decant your shampoo, face-cream, make-up remover and so on into small plastic bottles rather than take the full-size containers with you. You can buy little bottles from the chemist or save the ones supplied by hotels. Often, manufacturers produce 'trial sizes' of products which are ideal for taking away.

You can also purchase miniature versions of irons, hairdryers, heating elements, etc which are especially designed for travelling. Their small size in no way undermines their ability to do their job effectively and such items can be a godsend.

The items that are most cumbersome when it comes to packing are shoes and even one less pair will go a long way to lightening your load and relieving the pressure on space. However, this said, be sure to take one pair of shoes with you that are truly comfortable. Walking all day in shoes that hurt can be a nightmare.

THE ART OF PACKING

Extra Tips
1. Wrap anything which may leak in plastic bags before packing it.
2. Wrap shoes in plastic bags too — they may be dirty by the time you come to repack them at the end of your trip.
3. Take a bag for dirty laundry.
4. Pack crushable items at the last moment. Hang them up near your case and slip them in just before you leave.
5. Buy any books you want to read before you go off on your trip. Bookstalls at your point of departure may have a disappointingly limited selection. If you decide to take a 'serious' book with you, be sure to take something a little lighter too. You might need it to fall back on if the serious tome proves too hard going!

4.
COVERING FOR YOUR ABSENCE

IN THE OFFICE

Much as you would like to clear your desk before going away on a trip, this is seldom possible in practice. Often when time is short the temptation is to do the easy things first and leave those which require rather more effort or thought till last, which usually means they don't get done at all. Unfortunately, the 'difficult' pile will often contain some very pressing matters, at least some of which are bound to come to a head in your absence.

To avoid this happening, try an alternative approach. First, go through your outstanding tasks and divide them by priority into three piles:

COVERING FOR YOUR ABSENCE

(i) those tasks which must be done
(ii) those tasks which it would be helpful to complete but which could be left if time runs out
(iii) those tasks that can wait

Second, remove from all three piles anything straightforward which could be delegated to someone else. Then set aside pile (iii) and start work on pile (i) and, if time allows, tackle pile (ii).

Forward planning is essential, especially for women travelling frequently on business, or for prolonged periods. Somebody has to cover for you while you are away — preferably a secretary or assistant who works closely with you all of the time — but that person must be properly briefed on events so they are able to deal with any query or problem that might arise while you are away.

It is useful to make a list of what you anticipate happening during the period of your absence, together with the action you would want taken. If the person to whom you are delegating these tasks might need assistance, indicate which other people in the company could be approached for help. Note down the things you would like to be told about, or personally consulted on. If your secretary has recently started work for you, or if you are employing a temporary, you will need to leave specific instructions on dealing with your incoming mail — should everything just be acknowledged and await your return, or should some action be taken on telexes and letters which sound urgent? If you expect the latter, you must take time to brief the person as fully as possible and not expect them to know what to do automatically.

While you are away, your secretary or assistant will probably take the opportunity of carrying out administrative and organizational tasks (including the backlog of filing!) for which there is never time when you are around; if you have any reason to think that they might not get round to this of their own accord, you should indicate the jobs you would like to see done by the time you return. Your absences can also be a good time for

COVERING FOR YOUR ABSENCE

work to start on any restructuring of systems you have in mind.

Most importantly, don't forget to leave full details of your itinerary and contact address with telephone/telex/fax numbers with your own office. It is also useful to circulate this information to people in other departments who might need it urgently when people in your department are out to lunch, or gone for the day.

It will help you deal with the backlog of work when you do return to the office if you ask your secretary or whoever is covering for you to sort your incoming mail into three piles again:

(i)   matters requiring your urgent attention
(ii) non-urgent papers you can deal with in due course
(iii) things to read at your leisure

IN THE HOME

The key to avoiding chaos at home is anticipation: what is likely to happen or need attention in your absence, and what action do you need to take before you leave?

COVERING FOR YOUR ABSENCE

If you live alone, you obviously have to try to think of all eventualities, as everything is your own responsibility. Someone will have to be recruited to help out, preferably a neighbour or friend who lives nearby. Choose the most reliable person you can, which may not necessarily be your best friend. Even if you don't live alone, there are bound to be areas of day-to-day household management which are normally your responsibility and will not get done unless you make sure that someone you live with will take responsibility.

You are unlikely to forget to arrange for your plants to be watered or the cat to be fed, but the following list may alert you to other actions you need to take before going away to ensure everything runs smoothly in your absence.

1. Arrange for any bills to be paid in your absence. If you are going away for a long trip, you will need to arrange standing orders with your bank; for a shorter trip, you can either send off cheques to cover all your current bills before you leave or you can prepare all the envelopes, mark them with dates on which they are to be posted and give them to someone you can trust to put them in the post box at the appropriate time. Bills which arrive during your absence of anything up to three weeks can await your return. If you know that you will be receiving mail requiring attention whilst you are away, you will need to arrange for a trusted person to come in and open your post and take the appropriate action; this may mean leaving some signed cheques with that person, but make sure in any case that they have all the relevant documentation and know who to contact.

2. Make sure your home will be 'safe' in your absence. This is not only in terms of security — if you live alone, your home is probably doubly well secured anyway — but also in terms of possible problems caused by bad weather, notably burst pipes! Anna, who lives alone and travels frequently, tells a sorry tale of once coming back to find water gushing underneath her front door. She had not anticipated a cold spell and had left her house unheated

for two weeks. 'It was the most distressing thing that had ever happened to me,' she recalls. 'I've never seen such chaos — two ceilings had to come down and I had to have two rooms completely redecorated and new carpets.'

What precautions should you take? For a start check that your pipes are properly lagged. If you have central heating, you can set it to come on a couple of times — once in the middle of the night is a good idea — at a very low temperature, just to keep the house from freezing. Houses do retain warmth for some time, fortunately, as there are periods of several hours in the normal course of events when the temperature drops below freezing and they are unheated, during the night, or when you are out at work during the day; flats, of course, gain some warmth from adjacent flats. What is needed in order to prevent pipes freezing is a regular input of heat; what water pipes cannot sustain is long periods at sub-zero temperatures.

If you cannot achieve this, drain off your water tank entirely by turning the water off at the mains and leaving all taps running until the water has completely drained. Don't forget, though, to turn off the taps afterwards or you will find water gushing everywhere when you turn it back on.

3. Stop deliveries of milk and newspapers, both of which would otherwise betray your absence, and ask a neighbour to push your post through your letterbox. Many women feel it is a good idea to inform the police of any absence. It is certainly wise not to tell all and sundry of your precise plans to be away, as this information could be overheard by a would-be thief.

4. Check that you are properly insured to cover burglary and damage to your property in your absence. Some policies do not provide cover when the property is left empty for more than a certain length of time, but this is normally quite a long period and there should be no problem in relation to your absence on business trips or holidays. Check this point carefully, though, and ensure that the cover you have is adequate — there is nothing

COVERING FOR YOUR ABSENCE

worse than being under-insured!

5. Check your diary for any events which will take place in your absence — birthdays, weddings, etc, and at least prepare to get a card there on time. Once again, rather than posting these far too early, make the cards ready, mark the dates on which they should be sent and entrust them to someone to post. If you are keen for a present to arrive on the day rather than when you get back, you can, of course, prevail on the trusty friend again to deliver it. Another option is to have a gift sent by special delivery. Many good stores and a number of specialists shops will arrange for this. Flowers are, of course, always very welcome and easy to send.

If there will be an election during your absence and you wish to vote, don't forget to organize either a postal vote or appoint a proxy to vote on your behalf.

6. Last, but not least, make sure you leave details of where you can be contacted while you are away, plus telephone numbers of anyone who should be contacted in an emergency. If you have not already left a set of house keys with a friend or neighbour so they can water the plants or whatever, it might be worth leaving a set with a trusted person just in case your own set gets lost or stolen while you are away. The same applies to car keys.

5.
TAKING A POSITIVE APPROACH

When I asked the women who had agreed to be interviewed for this book what personal qualities they thought were the most important when it came to travelling as a lone woman, the one that was mentioned time and time again was self-confidence. Adaptability, stamina, a sense of humour all rated fairly high on the list too, but top of the list was without doubt the ability to keep a confident, positive outlook. Even the best planned trip will have its hitches, and it cannot be denied that difficulties that would seem fairly trivial at home can be magnified out of proportion when you are facing them alone, far away from home. But the secret is not to let things get you down — and not to let people put you down, a problem that women reported encountering far too often.

   Certainly those women who said they did not enjoy travelling — and there were quite a few who confessed that they found travelling alone an enormous strain — were more often than not the ones who also admitted to being low in self-confidence. Their lack of confidence led them to view a trip abroad with trepidation rather than enthusiasm and this meant that, although they were all good at their jobs, they failed to make the most of a trip in personal terms. But how do you develop a positive attitude?

TAKING A POSITIVE APPROACH

BE AN ASSERTIVE TRAVELLER

One way of tackling this problem is to make a conscious effort to build up your confidence, to set out to learn how to be, in the catch phrase of the moment, an 'assertive' traveller. Anne Dickson in her book *A Woman in Your Own Right* (Quartet, 1982) says that one of the definitions of being assertive is 'feeling confident in situations which you normally find intimidating'. There are very few women who could claim not to have experienced feelings of fear and anxiety, even panic, when embarking on their first few trips away on their own, but those who have travelled extensively and have come to really enjoy this part of their jobs, all say that what you need most to carry you through successfully is a combination of confidence and common sense. To get the most out of travelling you *have* to assert yourself.

Too often, women behave as 'passive' travellers — the ones who always get given the noisiest rooms in the hotel and the draughtiest tables in the restaurant because of their submissive attitude, or who return home having seen nothing of the places they have visited because they have been too nervous to explore. Either that, or they overcompensate for their feelings of intimidation and become aggressive and loud, antagonizing everyone around them and then being surprised and hurt by the hostility they encounter. Perhaps you recognize these two extremes in your own behaviour when you are put under the pressure of travelling alone? If you do, you are certainly not alone. Anne Dickson maintains that it is a common problem among women, this 'swing from aggression to passivity and back again' and that 'this to-ing and fro-ing in a cloud of uncertainty represents a major source of tension and discomfort'. The answer to this problem is to learn 'how to communicate our thoughts and feelings and needs, neither aggressively nor passively but assertively'.

There are lots of things that can go wrong on a trip and it is easy for your confidence to be undermined; maybe

TAKING A POSITIVE APPROACH

your travel arrangements do not work out as planned, or a business meeting goes badly, or perhaps you lose an item of your personal belongings or something is stolen, or you have an unpleasant encounter with someone. It takes time and experience to build up the level of confidence in yourself that allows you to brush off all adversity, but many women feel that it has been the very fact of travelling on their own which has enabled them to become confident and self-assured in a way that they would never have become otherwise.

It may not come naturally to you, but you must try to assert yourself and this starts from your deciding to put yourself first when you are out there on your own. Women often find this especially hard; we are so used to catering for the needs of others, putting them first, that putting your own needs and wants first is an alien form of behaviour. Travelling alone, you need to take the attitude that *you* matter most; you need to feel good, to get what you want, not to be put down by others. A confident, decisive approach will get you much further than being slightly apologetic about your requests or queries. Ignore sneering behaviour — you cannot be expected to know things that seem quite obvious to the person you are asking — how could you when you have just arrived? And don't take statements like, 'It's full already', or 'We don't have a reservation for you', or 'You can't do that' as absolute; challenge them, and you will be amazed what is actually possible.

- Arriving at a hotel in the USA recently after a transatlantic flight, the hotel had the correct reservation for one of our party of three, but, for two of us, the reservation commenced from the following night. 'Sorry', they said, 'we're absolutely full, you will have to stay somewhere else tonight and come back tomorrow.' In my early days of travelling, I probably would have done just that; on this occasion, however, I stood my ground. Speaking just loud enough so that other people in the reception area could hear, I announced that my

TAKING A POSITIVE APPROACH

companion and I had no intention of going elsewhere. As one of our party *did* have a reservation, it was quite clear that *they* had made a mistake about ours. I explained that we were tired after a long journey and therefore wanted our rooms right away. It worked — rooms were found immediately!

- On one of my first trips, I was travelling with another woman whose determined attitude I decided to take as a role model from then on. We arrived at Milan airport to be told the flight we were due to catch was overbooked and that we would have to catch another flight, maybe the next morning. I was already picking up my bags and sighing deeply when I heard her refusing point blank to accept this situation. 'Your airline has confirmed our reservations on this flight', she said 'and I insist that we get on it!' Sure enough we did.

- Having been 'bumped' from an internal flight in the USA on one occasion (protests to no avail this time!), I was offered hotel accommodation, sharing a room with a woman who was in the same predicament but who I did not know at all. Due to our insistence and perseverance, the airline finally offered us (a) a room each, (b) a taxi to the hotel, (c) dinner and (d) an overnight kit including toothbrush and toothpaste. It took a good half hour of negotiation, however, to get to what should have been offered in the first place.

Unfortunately, a woman is often seen as an 'easy touch' by hotels, airlines, etc; if they need to decrease their numbers for some reason they will often single out women, believing they will meet with less resistance, with little regard to the fact that it is women, particularly women on their own, who are put most at risk by their actions — trying to find alternative accommodation late at night or sleeping on an airport or bus station bench is very unpleasant and potentially dangerous.

You will often find that hotel staff are the worst offenders in undermining your confidence — they have a

TAKING A POSITIVE APPROACH

way of answering your questions which can make you feel absolutely stupid for asking, often acting in a superior manner, particularly if the hotel is a smart one. With time and practice, you will acquire the confidence to walk into any hotel in the world and not let anything about it phase you. In the meantime, you can take some positive steps to building up your confidence:

1. Remember that hotel staff are there for your convenience and if they are not making you feel at ease, they are not doing their job properly. It is also worth bearing in mind that most of them could not afford to stay in the hotels they work in and you can (even if you couldn't if you had to pay for yourself!), so they are in no position to look down their noses at you.

2. Do a lot of smiling. Smiling at people tends to ellicit pleasant reactions, even from a grumpy hotel receptionist.

3. If you are not getting answers to your questions, don't give up. Persevere until you find out what you wanted to know.

You MUST be here for the dental conference!

TAKING A POSITIVE APPROACH

4. Speak clearly and relatively loudly to avoid being asked to repeat what you have just said, which could make you more nervous.

If all this assertiveness doesn't sound very much like you, don't worry — it *will* come, and it need not manifest itself as aggression. Indeed you should try to prevent this happening, as aggression will not get you any further than shyness. What you are aiming for is confidence and self-assurance, not pushiness.

LEARNING TO LOVE YOUR OWN COMPANY

Another secret to developing a positive attitude is to learn to enjoy being by yourself, doing things alone. Many women tied to the domestic round would be deeply envious of the time you are able to spend alone — after all, how many opportunities do most people have to be truly on their own? Normally so many other people impose themselves on one's daily life as a matter of course — friends, family, colleagues — and so many demands are made for payments, decisions and acquiring the necessities of life. Travelling alone affords a golden opportunity to leave all of this behind. Although it may not always seem so if you are feeling a little depressed or lonely, the time spent alone is actually very precious and not a moment of it should be wasted. The more positively you can think about the opportunity of being yourself and catering only to your own needs, the more you will come to enjoy time spent alone.

For a start it gives you the chance to pamper yourself. In the privacy and comfort of your hotel room you can spend a whole evening — or two — concentrating on yourself. Linger for a long time in a luxurious foam bath, or spend time plucking your eye brows properly; treat yourself to a facial, a manicure, a pedicure or a leg wax; take along face packs, hair conditioners, all the kind of things you never have time for at home. Boost your ego by taking care with your appearance.

TAKING A POSITIVE APPROACH

Time spent alone is also the perfect time for thinking, planning, decision making. A whole range of thoughts will go through your mind, profound and not so profound, and it is well worth writing down some of the more useful ones, as they do seem to evaporate as quickly as they come! Many women recommend keeping a diary on a trip for just this reason.

Problems often seem clearer when you are distanced from them; you may have clear insights into the issues affecting your career or your personal life which are impossible when you are caught up in the daily round of either. The decisions you reach when you are travelling may not be implemented when you get back, but the opportunity to think things through will have been enormously valuable; you may, however, find yourself ready to make radical changes in your job or lifestyle — travelling may have given you just the new perspective you needed.

TAKING A POSITIVE APPROACH

Spending evenings alone

Business women face the prospect of evenings alone more often than women alone on holiday, simply because a day of appointments does not afford them the opportunity of meeting other people in the same boat. In some parts of the world, evening invitations are more common than others — in the USA, for example, you are much more likely to spend an evening with a business contact than you are in Europe, but it is still inevitable that at least some of your evenings will be spent on your own.

There is no doubt that long lonely evenings are the most difficult time for anybody travelling alone, but especially for women. Men have the opportunity of sitting around in bars or cafés without worrying; they can wander around late into the evening, taking in the ambience and sights. In many countries, women can do neither safely; even in countries where they can, they often feel uncomfortable, purely because of the possibility that they *might* be harassed. One woman, a banker, summed up this feeling rather well: 'I think every woman carries with her a whole emotional baggage of what has happened to her in the past, which makes it hard to relax; even minor incidents can ruin my enjoyment of sitting reading my newspaper in a bar. I find the constant threat of what men might do a terrible infringement on my privacy, even when it is an imagined rather than a real threat. In fact, even though I know I can deal with most situations that arise, I really resent having to. The art of putting people down was not a skill I *wanted* to acquire!'

One answer to the long lonely evening is to shorten it. Take a tip from many seasoned lone travellers, go to bed early and get up early. As Wendy, who has travelled alone extensively throughout the world, points out, 'Most places are at their best early in the morning — quiet, uncrowded, the light is often very good. If you are in a very hot country, this will be one of the cool parts of the day. It's a particularly good time to see places where the tourists will be flocking in droves later in the day before the crowds arrive. And you will be happy to have an early

TAKING A POSITIVE APPROACH

night if you have had a long day.' Another tip is to use the late afternoon/early evening — a time when it is generally much less risky to be a lone woman out and about — for exploring the sights. Once the day's engagements are over, get rid of your heavy bags, put on a pair of comfortable shoes and go out. Take advantage of shops, museums, galleries and so on which are still open, and of the fact that you *can* sit and enjoy a drink at this time of the evening with much less risk of being harassed than you can later on. On summer evenings, you can sit outside at a pavement café or terrace for an unhurried drink or two, or you can sit in a park or square and read for a while in many — though not all — countries. (Those where you can't, which include many of the Latin countries, are those whose male populations seem to think it is appropriate to pester women on their own, however, innocently. It will very soon become apparent to you whether this problem is going to arise in a particular place; the best advice then is to keep moving!)

TAKING A POSITIVE APPROACH

Another pleasant way of spending an evening alone is to attend a concert, the opera, the ballet or a similar cultural event. Hotels often provide a brochure containing details of what is going on that particular week, or local newspapers will tell you what is available. Going to the cinema alone is traditionally more difficult, though goodness knows why — why is it you are more likely to get a hand on your knee in a cinema than a theatre? However, many women do go to the cinema alone, and one who does offered the following advice, 'Arrive just before the film starts and leave promptly when it finishes. If someone does try to annoy you, move seats if at all possible, but if you cannot move because the cinema is full, make a rather loud comment to the offender so that everyone around you knows what is going on. That should put an end to the nuisance, even though you are not going to feel very comfortable about sitting next to him for the remainder of the film!'

Many women suggest travelling on to your next destination in the evening — provided that you have your accommodation booked, as turning up late at night without a reservation can be a recipe for disaster. Women who travel to the Scandinavian countries, for example, find this particularly appealing, as offices close relatively early, allowing adequate time to get to the airport and take the short flight onwards. Travelling within the USA, with its impressive network of internal flights, also lends itself to this approach. Travelling on in the evening avoids cutting into the following day and removes the possibility of being late at your first meeting because your plane was delayed, or you got stuck in rush-hour traffic coming in from the airport.

Eating alone

This is one activity about which many people seem to have a phobia, yet eating alone can be just as pleasurable as eating in company, provided you set about it with a positive attitude. If you really do not like to be *seen* to be eating alone, you would be best sticking to room service.

TAKING A POSITIVE APPROACH

Does MADAM require dessert or coffee?

Even this can be fun — having food delivered to your door and the dirty dishes removed without any effort asked of you is a luxury few people experience on a regular basis, and for many women makes a most enjoyable break from their normal routine.

If you are feeling more adventurous, there are an increasing number of restaurants these days that go out of their way to make the lone diner feel at ease. One useful piece of advice on this topic is offered by a teacher who travels regularly during her vacations — even if you are travelling on business, buy one of those travel guides that are the bible to the professional traveller (she specifically mentioned the travel guides in the 'Lonely Planet' series) and try out the eating places they recommend. Not only do you stand a better chance of being offered authentic local dishes at such restaurants, but they will also be used to travellers and are therefore more likely to be informal and welcoming. It also means you are likely to run into other lone travellers who will be eager to strike up a conversation.

TAKING A POSITIVE APPROACH

Unfortunately it is not impossible that you will come across restaurants who imply that they prefer not to serve unaccompanied women, or ones who make you feel uncomfortable by the way they treat you as a lone diner, relegating you to a pokey little table by the kitchen door and rushing you through your meal with unnecessary haste. What can you do? Remember to be assertive. Breeze in with a confident look and a cheery greeting, and ask for a table in a firm voice — a subtle hint that you are quite capable of creating a fuss if you do not get what you want — and don't be afraid to send the bill away if it arrives too early and unbidden. After all, you are the one who is paying.

MAKING THE MOST OF YOUR TRIP

Too often people do not make the best of the time they are away on a trip. They rush from one appointment to the next, thinking of little else but their work, blinkered to their surroundings, eating nothing but the 'international style' food offered in their hotel and then returning home without any feel for the places they have visited. As Jan, who works for a film company, confessed, 'I went to a dinner party just after returning from a trip and one of the other guests knew the city where I had been staying well. He kept asking me, "Did you see that?" "Did you go there?" and I hadn't done or seen any of the things he mentioned. I felt like a complete fraud — it was as if I hadn't really been there.'

Admittedly, if the trip is a short one, just a couple of days say, there will be little time for exploring or sightseeing, but if the trip is for longer it is usually possible to fit in some time for yourself as well fulfilling all your business engagements, as long as you have done some groundwork before you go.

Try to find out as much as possible about the places you will be visiting from books, magazines, other people who have been there. Learn something about their history, customs, major places of interest, specialities and so on

TAKING A POSITIVE APPROACH

and then earmark what you would most like to do, see, sample while you are there. You will probably find that you feel a great deal more enthusiastic about a trip if you approach it in this way.

Reading travel writing which relates to the area you are visiting is a particularly good way of whetting the appetite for a trip. The enthusiasm of a good travel writer is infectious and they usually offer insights into a country that cannot be found in the guide books. Christina Dodwell, Dervla Murphy, Freya Stark, Jan Morris and Paul Theroux are all writers who can conjure up a sense of adventure and express the sheer joy of travelling and exploring, regardless of whether they are writing about your particular destination.

Treat every trip as an opportunity that will never be repeated and pack in as much as you can. Select sights or events which really appeal to you — not just the ones the guide books say you should visit. Learning a few words of the language can help you to feel more at home and enable you to exchange a few words with the locals. Some women said they felt guilty if they went off sightseeing while on a business trip, that they were there to work, not enjoy themselves. But if you feel you are making the most of a trip in personal terms, you will find that you have even more energy and enthusiasm to put into your work. So try 'playing the tourist' in your spare time on a trip — take photographs, buy postcards and souvenirs for family and friends, and then you can share the experience on your return home. If you do, you will undoubtedly find yourself enjoying travelling more and more.

6.
COPING ALONE

Without any desire to be sexist, it has to be said that travelling alone is a completely different experience for a woman than for a man. Even if the woman is a high-powered executive, used to making crucial decisions all day, she may well still feel a tinge of anxiety about going down to the hotel bar for a drink on her own or out by herself to explore the sights — worries that are unlikely to trouble the average male travellers. Despite the much-debated liberation of Western woman, there is still a great deal of ambiguity in people's attitudes — including among women themselves — as to what exactly constitutes 'acceptable' behaviour in a woman. Add to this the underlying worry that most women have of being harassed by unwanted attention and the constant need to be aware of the possibility of danger, say from being out alone in an unfamiliar city at night, and it is no wonder that some women find travelling alone a nerve-racking exercise.

DEALING WITH UNWANTED COMPANY

Travel can, and will, provide you with some fascinating and valuable experiences, not least of which will be the people you meet along the way. I once met a man on a train journey who had just come back from a polar expedition and gave the most riveting account of his adventures. Similarly, Clare Francis now a best-selling author, then an intrepid lone yachtswoman, kept me spellbound during the lulls (of which there were many) at an exhibition I was helping to man on behalf of her then publishers. I wouldn't have minded running into *her* on a long journey!

COPING ALONE

Much as some of the people you meet will be fascinating, there are many people you will wish to avoid in the course of your travels. Women alone seem to attract the attention of others — whether it be sexual attentions, pure friendliness or attempts to find an easy target to bore rigid — and you will need to learn how to deal with people whose company you do not want. As one habitual lone traveller put it: 'My time abroad is far too precious to spend it with people I don't want to be with.'

You may find a change in your personality taking place over the course of various trips — you may become less outward or openly friendly, less willing to give others the benefit of the doubt, more suspicious. You will probably feel yourself becoming a tougher person. If this does happen to you, you are in good company — most women who gave me interviews for this book felt this had happened to them.

The best way to deal with unwanted advances is to nip them very firmly in the bud before the real trouble begins. Most women I spoke to were all too familiar with the 'Can I join you?' syndrome at dinner and recommended that trying to act confidently and in a self-contained manner often worked as a positive deterrent. If you needed props to achieve this, be sure to have a book, or some notes or work with you. Most important, avoid looking round nervously.

In any situation where casual conversation seems to be leading to possible sexual overtures you don't welcome, it is far wiser to make your displeasure known immediately with an overt snub than to deal with a situation turned sour later on. Many women arrive at these situations through sheer politeness, a desire not to offend or to be thought of as snooty; the benefit of the doubt is often given because the man, after all, might just want some friendly conversation and, in any case, you will feel very silly if you were wrong. Have no such scruples! Better by far to give verbal offence to someone who will get over it rather quickly than to suffer verbal or even physical abuse yourself, which you will find takes a little longer to fade from the memory.

COPING ALONE

A number of women warned against certain innocent actions that men can sometimes misread as encouragement, for instance:

Don't let someone who you don't know treat you to meals, entertainment, etc, otherwise they may feel you owe them something. Always pay your own way.

Don't accept lifts or offers to show you around from men you do not know well, unless you are absolutely sure the intention is honourable.

When lost and poring over your streetmap, ask a woman, or group of people, to help you find the way; men have sometimes been known to read meanings you never intended into an innocent request for directions.

Pam, a fashion executive from London, tells how she had a seemingly innocent encounter — with a sting in the tail! On a trip to Iceland, a man asked if he could join her at dinner; she was in a sociable mood, so agreed, and a thoroughly pleasant evening of conversation resulted, with no hint of it turning into anything more. Pam came away feeling how nice it was that one could spend an evening enjoying a man's company without ending up fending off unwanted advances. It quite restored her faith in human nature. Then the letters started arriving. She told me, 'He had been so pleasant! We had showed each other pictures of our respective families — I gave him my business card and said if he and his family were ever in London, they should look me up and I would show them round. Imagine my horror when he wrote and told me he couldn't get our meeting out of his mind, he had become completely infatuated with me, apparently. He was threatening to come to London and pursue our romance! I got very worried about this — explaining him away to my boyfriend would have made an interesting story. Then the letters started to become quite obscene, which really upset me, as I couldn't square that with the way he had behaved when we met. Of course, he never did come to London and the letters stopped after a while, but it has

COPING ALONE

made me much more cautious about letting people know how to contact me!'

In fact, preserving one's anonymity is advice given out by many travellers. If you *do* feel you want to give your address to people you meet casually whilst travelling, give a business address if you have one; as Pam's story shows, it will not assure you complete immunity, but imagine how much worse it would have been if those letters had started turning up at her home! The feeling that someone can get to you in your own home is a very disturbing one, so be very reticent about giving this information. If someone is pressing you to give your address, and you cannot quite bring yourself to refuse outright, have no scruples about making something up if you have any reason at all to doubt their motives. Be similarly cautious about giving out your last name — particularly if you are listed in the telephone directory at home!

A little cautious behaviour in your hotel does no harm; keep the number on your room key out of view and when the waiter asks your room number, discreetly show him the key rather than saying the number out loud. Avoid carrying a file or case with your name prominently displayed — hotel staff are not supposed to give out guests' room numbers for obvious security reasons, but it is not unknown for them to do so. Being pursued to your hotel room is thankfully not a common occurrence, but it *can* happen (and has to one woman I know), so extremely simple precautions can prevent it ever happening to you.

Of course, encounters with men can provide some good dinner party stories after the event! Staying in a hotel in Spain, Melissa was absolutely amazed when a man made a pass at her in the lift; but she fended him off fairly easily. The next morning, she arrived at her first meeting of the day, ready to recount her story to her clients, and who should be sitting behind the desk ...

SEX AND THE SINGLE TRAVELLER

The popular image of a man away on a business trip or convention is of a person constantly on the look out for a bit of 'the other'; how fair an image this is is hard to tell, particularly as men are not usually in the habit of bragging to women about their sexual exploits. What is apparent, talking to women whose husbands or lovers travel, is that they do worry about this every time their partner goes away — even some women who feel extremely confident in the partner's fidelity admit to wondering if a chance opportunity provided by travel would not be taken.

So, do women who travel behave in the same way as they imagine men do? I asked all the women I interviewed in my research for this book about their attitude to casual sexual encounters when travelling alone. I divided the responses into those from women who were happily married or in steady relationships and those who had no current relationship or whose relationship was in trouble, on the assumption that the two groups would act differently.

The former group appear, unlike the picture we have of their male counterparts, to be a faithful bunch! With very few exceptions, women with steady partners at home said they never had casual affairs whilst away on a trip; they certainly were not looking out for men and, if advances were made by someone they found attractive, they would definitely resist, although many admitted to being tempted. The reasons for resisting are summed up rather well by Sarah who works for a large multi-national, 'When I travel I feel that Steven needs to be sure he can trust me absolutely — that's part of the deal. If things were reversed, I would hate to have to worry about what he might be up to. So no casual relationship would be worth the betrayal of his trust, however much fun it might be at the time.' Guilt seems to stand in the way of some women submitting to temptation; others simply did not feel any inclination to sleep with anyone but their partner — 'Why on earth should I want to do that?' was an utterance I heard more than once in the course of my questioning, and I must say that my small cross-section of society seemed to support the theory that women are more monogamous than men.

Of the women with steady partners who *had* had affairs, all were adamant that they would never tell their partner about it; again, betrayal of trust was the important factor in their decision not to do so. Some were glad that they had had the experience and others felt their 'guilty secret' weighed heavily upon them. Fiona told me, 'I had three wonderful days in Copenhagen with a man I was never going to see again. I have never regretted it and, because it was, in a way, outside of reality for me, I don't feel it has anything to do with my relationship with my husband.' This feeling that what happens to you when you are travelling has nothing to do with real life was one that was expressed frequently.

Some women, who would not go as far as having a casual physical relationship, did admit to 'romantic' encounters which they enjoyed and allowed to progress much further than they would if they were on home ground. From all accounts, travelling can make you feel a little schizophrenic — it seems that being in a different place can make you feel like a different person. You may

COPING ALONE

also feel more vulnerable than usual and consequently more open to approaches from men you find attractive than you might normally be. Indeed, many cities seem to demand a little romance — a mood may be created that you can slip into all too easily if the opportunity arises. Free from the shackles of your real existence, you can accept the dinner invitation which would be out of the question on your home territory, simply because the implications of the relationship continuing could not be contemplated. When you are travelling the romance is finite and under control; it can boost your ego without your having anything to feel guilty about later.

However, beware that this does not backfire on you. One woman who works for a television company recounted how she had become very friendly with a man who worked in an overseas branch of her company and had let the relationship develop much further than she would have done had they been colleagues at home. Of course, being alone when she visited his branch office gave her the opportunity of accepting his invitations to dinner and she spent several evenings in his company. They were very attracted to each other, but stopped short of a physical relationship. Then, quite out of the blue, he was transferred home and they found themselves working alongside each other. She now finds the fact that they didn't have an affair in the physical sense an enormous relief; their flirtation is something they can look back on with affection — and some amusement — without embarrassment.

Guilt feelings over an illicit affair can endure for quite a time, even when back home and into the old routine again. One woman said, 'It wasn't so much what my husband would think if he knew, but what my *children* would think. That made me feel awful. I hadn't thought of them at all when I was in the throes of the affair. I suppose it wouldn't have fitted in with my sexual image of myself at the time to think of myself as wife and mother of three.'

Regaining the sexuality you feel has taken such a battering at the hands of family life can be a powerful motivation towards having a fling. Travelling on your own, you suddenly have the opportunity to spend time on your personal appearance — you dress smartly, you spend time over your make-up and hair, you rediscover yourself as an attractive woman. You are so immersed in your role as wife and mother that you are amazed — and immensely flattered — that anyone should find you attractive, even sexy. For many, the flattery itself is enough — they don't need the affair, just the boost of feeling desirable.

Women who are footloose and fancy free have different stories to tell, as you would imagine, and many take full advantage of the 'anonymity' travel affords them. They positively thrive on knowing that they will probably never see the person again after the parting of the ways, and make the most of the fact that a casual affair whilst travelling is not going to impinge on 'real' life. It is quite common for women to feel they are a different person when they travel, who does quite different things from their regular persona. Travel *is* a great escape from routine, from everyday life and everyone knows it cannot last, so no wonder our behaviour patterns seek a bit of escapism too! Acting uncharacteristically on holiday or on a business trip is extremely usual and you are not the only one if it happens to you!

If I had been writing this book ten years ago, more recently than that perhaps, women would, no doubt, have been extolling the joys of casual partners on trips to a greater extent than they do today. However, the spread of AIDS has frightened many women considerably, making them much more cautious and causing many to abandon sex other than with regular partners. Of course, sexual infections have always been with us, but the deterrent factor of AIDS has been far more apparent than the possibility of contracting a venereal disease which can be treated, thankfully, at the end of the day. Women I know, who freely admit to several sexual relationships during their travels in the Seventies, would not contemplate acting in the same way in the Eighties.

COMMON SENSE AND SELF-DEFENCE

Protecting your belongings

It is common sense not to carry valuables around with you unless you cannot avoid doing so. Whenever possible leave items such as your passport, excess travellers' cheques, airline tickets and so on, in the hotel's safety deposit box and only take those things which you are sure you will need.

Obviously there are going to be times when you have to take everything with you and these are the times when you must be extra cautious and alert. Try to be aware at all times of where your valuables are. Keep your handbag or other valuables in sight or touch. If you have put your handbag on the floor in a restaurant, keep your foot against it so you can feel the moment somebody tries to grab it; better still, wrap the strap around your ankle; best of all, try to find an alternative to the floor! *Never* hang a handbag or jacket containing valuables on the back of your chair — this is making it really easy for the thief.

Women who are cautious are hardly ever the ones to suffer thefts of personal items; thieves seem to prey on those who are rather careless with their belongings, who go around with open handbags (just to make things really easy, the purse is usually at the top and sticking at least half way out!), who never know where they have put their passport or credit cards, and don't even miss them until several days later, by which time the thief has had a field day. If you are not a naturally cautious person, you will need to train yourself to be more so — after all, if that bag is stolen, there goes your means of travel, your ability to pay for anything, your contact with the rest of your world, i.e. your address book!

Women living in New York have to be very street-wise indeed, and I am sure it is they who originated the practice of wearing the shoulder strap of their handbag across the body, with the handbag itself towards the front. It is very difficult for your bag to be stolen if you wear it this way and it leaves you with both hands free. Also, if you do use a shoulder bag, be sure to walk on the inside of the pavement. In many Mediterranean countries thieves have taken to their motorbikes and cruise up and down the pavement's edge looking for a suitable bag to snatch. Before you realize what has happened, the thieves have disappeared into the traffic.

If someone does try to grab your bag, remember the golden rule: do not resist. The automatic reaction is to hang on and fight back, but this can be dangerous. In some parts of the world, from Los Angeles to Nairobi, life is held cheap and any resistance from you could change a thief into an attacker. So hand over your possessions on request; you can replace your handbag and money but not your life.

What to do

If your passport is lost or stolen   Contact the local police and inform them of the theft or loss as quickly as possible. Next you will have to arrange for a replacement passport or emergency travel documents through your nearest embassy or consulate. This will be much easier and quicker if you have taken the precaution of keeping a note of your passport number and details somewhere safe.

If your travellers' cheques are lost or stolen   Hopefully you will have kept a note of the serial numbers of the cheques. If you suspect that they have been stolen contact the local police. Many of the companies which issue travellers' cheques have offices abroad and should be able to issue you with replacement cheques quickly.

If you credit cards are lost or stolen   Telephone, fax or telex the credit card company as soon as possible and inform them of the loss. It will be a great help if you have kept a record of the card number(s). Again, inform the local police if you think that your cards were stolen and ask them for written confirmation of your report.

Protecting yourself

Most of the time, in most places in the world, you will be perfectly safe, providing you take reasonable care and are sensible about avoiding areas that are known to be potentially dangerous. Some countries are obviously more hazardous than others for a lone woman traveller, and every city in the world has areas where it would be foolhardy to wander alone at night. Wherever you are — be it Paris, Sydney, New York or Timbuctoo — your common sense will tell you to avoid unpopulated, badly lit streets after dark and to be generally vigilant when out alone. For most women these days, such precautions are instinctive.

When travelling alone you should adopt a sensible, cautious approach to the possibility of danger, without becoming paranoid. Do not walk around feeling frightened, but be aware of situations and people. Let this become second nature to you and you will find that reasonable caution does not impinge on your enjoyment, or, indeed, on your freedom. One woman who travels alone frequently for a merchant bank said that she always takes stock of people in close proximity to her: walking along a rather empty street, she will glance to see who is behind, and cross the road if she feels the situation merits it; entering a railway carriage she will observe if there is a corridor; if not, she looks to see who is already there. If it is a single man or group of men she does not like the look of, she will choose an alternative carriage. If it is *empty*, she may also decide to move, particularly if she is travelling out of normally busy periods — she does not, after all, know who will get on at the next stop! Rather than exhibiting paranoia, she is exercising instant judgements on people based on a variety of experiences, good and bad. You will also need to make summary judgements, which will not, at least on your first few journeys alone, be backed up by experience. But erring on the side of caution never did anyone any harm, whereas hesitating to act because you feel your suspicions are ridiculous could cost you dear. Fortunately, many women are extremely intuitive and can gain a fast impression of a person's intentions from a single look. No doubt this is part of our in-built survival kit.

Talking to numerous women about avoiding the sort of situations which have their roots in sexual harassment, however mild or serious, one particular comment is made time and time again: that it is the way that *you* come across to other people that really controls events. If you are naturally a rather open, welcoming sort of person with broad smiles for the world at large, you are, unfortunately, going to have to make some changes. All the women I have asked have said that over the years they have adopted a confident, self-contained attitude; they are friendly but not over-inviting. Some would even say they look 'fierce' or 'forbidding', though this is maybe taking things a bit

COPING ALONE

far. In other words, body language is used to say, 'I'm quite all right on my own, thank you', 'Yes, I *would* rather read my book', 'I really *do* know my way around' and a whole variety of other signals. Women who travel frequently alone try not to dither, they do not pore over street maps in deserted places or late at night; they proceed purposefully and give the impression of knowing exactly what they are doing, even if the opposite is true.

Women often find themselves in dangerous circumstances because they have taken a risk as a way of getting out of a frustrating situation. Usually these situations relate to getting somewhere rather than hanging around and result in walking alone down deserted streets at night; or accepting lifts from strangers, or taking 'taxis' which are not really taxis at all — even if no actual danger ensues from doing this, you can almost guarantee an exorbitant fare; or hitching a lift; or even accepting offers of accommodation from strangers. Quite clearly, we would all maintain that any of these actions are foolhardy and we would never do them. In reality there is hardly a woman who will not be forced to admit that she has not done at least one of them in her travelling experience. Fortunately I have yet to encounter anyone who has come to real harm, but the near-miss stories are numerous. Even so, the advice must be *steer clear of risky situations*, however inconvenient the alternatives may seem at the time.

Self-defence

A woman is unlikely to get the better of a persistent male attacker in a physical confrontation. For this reason avoidance is by far the best tactic; don't take risks or look for confrontations. Equally, if you are attacked, your aim should always be to escape, not to fight back — follow the old school of thought and 'shout at the top of your voice and run like hell'. Shouting is a way of distracting your assailant, putting him off guard just long enough to win yourself the precious few seconds that might enable you to run away.

Personal alarms work the same way, and more and more women have taken to carrying these with them. Typically they are the size of a pack of cards, battery operated, and double as a torch and a piercing alarm which serves to put an attacker off-guard, allowing time for you to escape or summon help. Many of these alarms are equipped with an attachment which allows them to be fitted into the door jamb of your hotel room, providing additional security to the often flimsy lock.

Women who carry personal alarms seem to do so chiefly for the psychological comfort they derive from knowing the alarm is to hand. Indeed, one woman who also lives alone tells me that she keeps hers by her bedside all the time. Having your alarm ready in your hand when you are walking alone, particularly after dark, makes many women feel all the better for knowing they can startle a potential attacker. However, do remember that personal alarms do not afford you a cloak of invulnerability, and that avoiding any potentially hazardous situations is always the best course to take. Also remember if you do use the alarm, do not stand there holding it. Your attacker

COPING ALONE

may quickly recover from his surprise and try again. Set the alarm off, then throw it towards your attacker and run for the nearest well-lit street or populated place. If you think you are being followed, don't be afraid to walk into a bar, petrol station or any other public place and ask for help or call the police.

Unless you are trained in the art of self-defence and very athletic, it is unlikely that you will have much chance of immobilizing an attacker, but there are one or two techniques you could use to try and wind him or cause him pain so that his attention is diverted just long enough for you to escape. Only resort to these methods if you feel that there is no other means of escape; the danger is that if you hurt your attacker without persuading him to release his grasp you may just goad him into more violent action than he might otherwise have taken.

If an attacker grabs you from *behind*, you can:

1. Stamp as hard as you possibly can on the top of his foot; this is particularly effective if you are wearing shoes with pointed heels.

2. Bring your arm forward and then hit him with as much force as you can muster in the stomach with your elbow. This might just wind him, forcing him to loosen his hold and giving you the chance to run off.

3. Kick backwards aiming at the bony part on the front of the shin, or scrape your shoe down this part of his leg. This can be extremely painful.

If you are attacked from the *front*, you can:

1. Kick with your full force at the front of his shin or the side of his knee. Don't try for the traditional target — his testicles — as you are unlikely to succeed in executing the kick without the attacker grabbing your leg first; or if he is wearing a coat or long jacket, these will cushion your blow.

2. Grab for one of his ears and twist, again this is very painful and may force the attacker to let go of you so you can escape.

3. Flatten out straight the fingers of one hand and, keeping them rigid, jab them into his throat.

4. Using two fingers, jab his eyes hard. Don't be squeamish about doing this — your safety is too important.

Hopefully you will never need to resort to such methods of defending yourself, especially if you take sensible precautions to stay out of danger in the first place.

7. TRAVEL AND YOUR HEALTH

SENSIBLE HEALTH PRECAUTIONS

Vaccinations

If you are planning a trip anywhere outside Europe or North America, you need to find out well in advance of your departure — six to eight weeks beforehand if possible — whether or not you will require immunization for the country or countries to which you are travelling. Advice on immunization is readily available from good travel agents and airlines. The regulations are constantly changing but the airlines tend to keep up to date on the immunization rules for all countries because they are legally obliged to fly you home free of charge if you cannot produce evidence of having received the relevant vaccinations. Many countries on the African continent, for instance, require a certificate to show vaccination against yellow fever before they will allow entry. You might need vaccinations against a number of diseases for some countries. Not all these can be done in one go, so again it is important to check out well in advance of your departure exactly what is required.

Vaccinations can be done either by your doctor or at a vaccination centre (your doctor will be able to tell you where the nearest one of these is). In Britain, the vaccination centre will supply you with a stamped, internationally recognized certificate of vaccination immediately. If your doctor does the vaccination you will have to take the certificate along to your local DHSS office for stamping.

Main diseases and precautions

Disease	Areas of risk	Means by which it is caught	Vaccination
Cholera	Africa, Asia, Middle East	Contaminated food or water	2 injections 1-2 weeks apart
Malaria	Africa, Asia Central and S. America	Bite from infected mosquito	None, but anti-malarial tablets available
Polio	Everywhere except Australia, New Zealand, Europe and N. America	Direct contact with infected person	3 doses of drops at 4-8 week intervals
Typhoid	As for polio, i.e. conditions of poor hygiene and sanitation	Contaminated food, water or milk	2 injections at 4-6 weeks apart; can be reduced to 10 days
Yellow Fever	Africa and S. America	Bite from infected mosquito	1 injection at a Yellow Fever Vaccination Centre at least 10 days before departure

*Adapted from leaflet SA35, issued by the DHSS for UK Health Departments

TRAVEL AND YOUR HEALTH

Travellers are no longer required to have smallpox vaccinations as it is now considered that the threat of smallpox has been eliminated worldwide.

It would be wise to ask your doctor if your destination poses any particular health risks. Although the regulations may not require immunization against particular diseases for travel in some countries, it might still be sensible to get cover in certain instances simply in terms of your own safety. Your doctor will also be able to warn you about possible side effects from the vaccinations, another reason why you should be sure to check immunization regulations out well in advance. Some people do react to the vaccines, occasionally being quite poorly, and you do not want to embark on a trip feeling under the weather.

Malaria

If you are planning to travel in a tropical country you are particularly at risk from malaria, so be sure to ask your doctor about anti-malarial tablets. You usually have to start taking the tablets several days before travelling, continue to take them throughout the time of your visit and then carry on with them for a month after your return.

Avoiding mosquito bites

Malaria is spread by mosquitoes, as is yellow fever, so it is imperative to take precautions against mosquito bites. Even in countries where malaria or yellow fever are not a risk, mosquitoes can be troublesome, giving painful and sometimes disfiguring bites to any exposed part of the anatomy. Always take a suitable insect repellent with you on your trip; do not rely on buying one at your destination or you might have been bitten before you get round to it. Your chemist can advise on which repellents are most effective. Other important precautions are to keep your legs and arms covered when outside in the evening, sleep under a mosquito net and either spray an insecticide or use a mosquito coil in your room at night. Mosquitoes

TRAVEL AND YOUR HEALTH

dislike draughts, so try to get air-conditioned accommodation wherever possible.

Food and drink

Contaminated food and drink can cause a wide variety of unpleasant and occasionally serious diseases, so it is well worth being very careful to avoid any food or drink which might pose the threat of infection. Here are a few tips on how to minimize the risks:

Avoid tap water unless you are sure it is safe. Either use bottled water or sterilize your water with water purifying tablets — these are available from chemists and should be considered an essential part of your luggage on most trips abroad. You can also boil your water to make it safe, if you have the necessary equipment, such as a travel

TRAVEL AND YOUR HEALTH

'element', to do this. Remember, though, that the water must boil vigorously for five minutes.

Don't forget about ice too. You may have been rigidly disciplined about your drinking water and then overlook that the ice cubes in your gin and tonic will have been made with tap water. Always ask for your drinks to be brought without ice in such cases. It is even advisable to purify the water you use for cleaning your teeth.

Avoid milk unless it has been well boiled before use, or has been pasteurized or sterilized. Stick to black tea and coffee if in doubt.

Avoid underdone meat or fish

Avoid reheated foods — freshly cooked foods are generally much safer. This is one reason to opt for the busy restaurant; the turnover of food will be more rapid and you are much less likely to be given something which has been standing around or reheated.

Avoid eating anywhere there are lots of flies — flies are the primary carriers of disease and move happily between rubbish tip and restaurant kitchen.

Take care with foods which have a short life such as seafood, cream and ice cream.

Take care with uncooked foods such as salads and uncooked fruit — who knows if they have been washed in contaminated water? If you want fresh fruit, peel it yourself.

Be prepared for common complaints

There cannot be many travellers who have not succumbed at some time or other to the dreaded *traveller's diarrhoea*, otherwise known as a Montezuma's Revenge, Delhi Belly, Rangoon Runs and many other names depending on where you happen to be. If you do fall prey to 'the runs', don't eat anything for 24 hours, but drink plenty of liquids as diarrhoea has the effect of dehydrating your body. If the local water is not drinkable, use bottled water

TRAVEL AND YOUR HEALTH

instead. Fruit juice and tea or coffee should be avoided as they act as irritants to the lining of the stomach and so will only exacerbate the problem.

Should you fall victim to a bout of severe diarrhoea, your body will dehydrate and you will need to take steps to rehydrate yourself, particularly if you are in a hot climate. If you are travelling to a country where you know diarrhoea is bound to strike unless you are exceptionally lucky, such as India or Mexico, take with you some rehydration sachets which you can mix with bottled or purified water. Alternatively you can improvise and make your own rehydrating draught with the following:

1 litre purified or bottled water
1/2 teaspoon salt
4 heaped teaspoons of sugar, glucose or honey

As far as a simple dose of the 'runs' are concerned, there are plenty of good proprietary remedies on the

TRAVEL AND YOUR HEALTH

market. Traveller's diarrhoea has provided a growing business for the drug companies over the years and they have obviously found it well worth spending considerable amounts on research, with the result that many of the drugs currently available are effective and quick-acting. You will certainly need to choose one which will stop the condition in its tracks if you are to get through your schedule or be able to travel. Your chemist can give you good advice on what to choose, or consult your doctor if you have a particularly sensitive stomach — but do this *before* you travel. Given how often this complaint strikes the traveller, it is wise to carry suitable medicines whenever you go abroad.

If the condition persists for more than a couple of days and proprietary medicines do not seem to be working, you must consult a doctor as you could be facing a more serious, viral form of diarrhoea which requires different treatment.

Headaches, colds and flu can strike just as easily in Greece as in Greenwich, so do not forget to take some suitable medicines with you. Take supplies of whatever pain-killer you normally use at home, such as paracetamol, aspirin, etc. These sorts of drugs can be very expensive abroad. For colds and flu, if you are keeping up with a busy timetable and seeing clients, the remedies that suppress the symptoms for a number of hours at a time might be the best choice, though watch for side effects with these.

If you are not used to hot, humid conditions, you may be susceptible to a number of conditions provoked by heat. The obvious ones are *sunburn and sunstroke*; or at least they would be obvious if you were going on holiday but are often overlooked by the working woman who feels she will not have a free moment for any sunbathing. You can in fact get badly burned in a number of unexpected situations, such as sitting outdoors for a meal in a restaurant, or waiting for a bus or taxi. If you are travelling somewhere hot, take suntan lotion or cream with you and apply it to exposed areas of skin regularly, just to be safe. Even better, wear a sun hat.

Heat and humidity can also trigger *thrush* or *cystitis*. If you know you are susceptible to these complaints, take suitable medication with you. Both conditions can make your life a misery and it may be embarrassing and expensive to acquire suitable treatment abroad. All women travelling in hot sticky climates should wear cotton underwear and be scrupulous about personal hygiene to lessen the risk of such problems arising. It is also worth avoiding tight trousers or jeans, especially when travelling, for the same reasons.

Don't forget your *teeth*. A visit to your dentist before you travel, particularly if you are experiencing the slightest problem with your teeth, can avoid a great deal of trouble and expense later. Dental care can be extremely costly abroad.

Finally if you are taking any medication regularly — the *contraceptive pill* for example — be sure you have adequate supplies for the duration of your trip. Keep all such medications in your hand luggage when travelling, just in case your other luggage goes astray en route.

THE TRAVELLER'S FIRST AID KIT

Whenever you travel abroad it is advisable to take a small first aid kit with you, so you can treat yourself if you should suffer any minor injury or complaint. The list below covers the essential items:

Antiseptic wipes
Antiseptic cream
Packet of different sized plasters
A crepe bandage
Tweezers
Small pair of scissors
Paracetamol (or the pain-killer of your choice)
Antihistamine cream for insect bites or stings
Water sterilizing tablets
Remedy for diarrhoea and sickness

TRAVEL AND YOUR HEALTH

Extras you can add to this list include:

Medication for any complaints to which you know are susceptible; eg an anti-fungal cream for thrush or pills for hay fever if you know you will suffer in certain conditions
Cold and flu remedy
Laxatives
Indigestion tablets
Lip balm (for chapped lips)
Sunburn cream
Pills for travel sickness
Multivitamin pills (if you feel your diet might be inadequate)
STs or tampons — the upheaval of travelling can sometimes trigger an unexpected period

MEDICAL INSURANCE

Whenever you travel abroad you should be sure you have adequate insurance cover for medical expenses. Your company may attend to this on your behalf or you might find you need to make the arrangements yourself. Even if your company is dealing with the matter, make sure you know the details of the policy so that you can be assured that the cover it offers is sufficient.

How much cover you need depends on the country to which you are travelling and your own age and medical condition. Bills for hospital treatment, should you be unfortunate enough to require it, can be very large. If you are travelling to North America, bear in mind that the cover you will require for this is much greater than elsewhere; medical treatment in the USA and Canada is extremely expensive. You will also need cover for visits to a doctor, medicines and dental treatment. Insurance can be obtained from travel agents, motoring organizations, banks and insurance companies and they can usually advise you on the best type of policy for your requirements and travel plans.

TRAVEL AND YOUR HEALTH

Britain does have reciprocal health agreements with a number of countries. Free or reduced health care is available for British citizens in all countries that are members of the EEC, many other Western European countries, some Eastern Bloc countries and in countries such as Hong Kong and New Zealand. The details of the entitlements varies from country to country; all the relevant information is contained in a leaflet produced by the DHSS called 'Medical Costs Abroad' (leaflet SA30).

Most EEC countries require that you produce a special form, known as form E111, when claiming your right to medical treatment. This has to be obtained from the DHSS *before* you go away. Other countries ask for your passport to establish your entitlement to free or reduced treatment.

Many insurance companies recommend taking out extra medical insurance even if you are travelling to a country with which Britain has a health agreement, as the cover offered by these agreements is usually restricted; for instance, it only covers treatment in the state hospitals, which in places like Greece may be of a poor standard, and it does not cover the cost of flying you home if you are ill.

If you are pregnant and travelling, check that the insurance policy does not have pregnancy exclusions. Some companies will not pay any claims resulting from pregnancy; others will not pay if you were pregnant when you took the policy out. Again, make sure you are adequately covered before leaving home.

Insurance tips

1. Always get a receipt for any payment you have to make. Bills for hospital treatment are usually settled at a later date directly by the insurance company, but bills for seeing a doctor or dentist or any medicines usually have to be paid for immediately. Sending receipts in with a claims form on your return speeds up payment and prevents any quibbling.

TRAVEL AND YOUR HEALTH

2. Take a copy of your policy with you and leave a photocopy of it at home. Sometimes only the original document will be accepted.

3. Check what the procedure is for making a claim. Some companies ask you to claim immediately, say by telephone, rather than waiting until you return home.

4. Do not forget your E111 certificate if it is relevant to your trip. Take the accompanying DHSS leaflet along too so you can check your entitlements.

5. Check the exclusion clauses in the insurance policy — all the things for which you cannot claim — *before* setting off on your trip.

6. If you do need treatment while abroad and are presented with a large bill and have inadequate funds to meet it you can call on your company for assistance if you are travelling on their business or, if you are travelling independently, you can contact your own bank at home to ask for money; if that all fails, contact your nearest consulate.

TRAVEL SICKNESS

This problem is much easier to prevent than treat, so take a suitable tablet before you travel if you are prone to travel sickness — don't wait and see if you will suffer or not. Most tablets need to be taken at least half an hour before you depart. Ask your chemist to recommend one that is less likely to cause drowsiness, as this can be unpleasant and even dangerous if you are driving. Forms of transport most commonly causing travel sickness are: older buses travelling on rough roads; boats, particularly smaller ones without stabilizers, but almost any boat when the sea is rough; hovercraft. Modern cars and coaches travelling on tarmac roads do not usually present a problem but, if you are susceptible, try to sit in the front seat of the car and avoid the back part of the coach.

TRAVEL AND YOUR HEALTH

Aircraft, now that they fly way above the weather, seldom create any problems, except in cases of prolonged turbulence or if you are a very nervous flier.

If you have not taken a tablet beforehand and start to feel ill, the first thing to try is taking in some fresh air. Open the window if you are in a motor vehicle, go up on deck if you are on a boat, or turn one of the overhead ventilators towards your face on an aircraft. Keep your head still and eyes shut in order to control the effect of motion and breathe deeply.

The movement of a car, boat or plane can make you feel sick because it upsets the delicate relationship between the messages sent by the eye and those sent by the ear. Normally, the eye takes in information about the position of your body and feeds it to your brain; at the same time there is a mechanism in the inner ear which controls your sense of balance and this too feeds information about the position of your body, at every moment, to the brain. The trouble starts when the messages that are sent by the eye do not match those sent by the ear. Result: nausea. This is why closing your eyes — cutting out the messages sent by the eye — and keeping your head still — giving the ear a chance to correct its balance mechanism — may help reduce the feelings of sickness.

Other tips for coping with travel sickness are:

1. Make sure you are not sitting in a smoking area; the smell of smoke can make you feel much worse.
2. Don't eat a large meal before setting off on a trip, or consume any alcohol.
3. Don't read a book or try to write while travelling in a car; look out of the window and concentrate on the far horizon instead.
4. Do drink small amounts — of non-alcholic drinks — often.
5. Do eat a small meal — something easily digested — before a trip. An empty stomach exacerbates the sensations of nausea. Sweet foods during the trip can also make some people feel less nauseous.

6. Try and go to sleep; this gives the eye and the ear — and therefore your brain — a rest!

These suggestions may help reduce the sensations of nausea, but if you know you are prone to travel sickness, or feel that there might be any risk of it, the only really sure way of countering it is to take a suitable travel sickness pill before you start your journey. Feeling sick all through a journey is utterly miserable.

If you are pregnant, check with your doctor which types of travel sickness pills are safe for you to take.

AVOIDING JET LAG

Nobody who travels frequently can deny the enormous benefits of air travel — it is quick, efficient and remarkably safe compared with other forms of transport. However, the very fact that we can be transported so rapidly over vast distances — through time zones, from hot to cold, day to night — is bound to cause our bodies some confusion. Our minds can cope with the concept of Concorde, for example, making it possible for us to leave London and arrive in New York an hour before we left, but our bodies take a little longer to catch on. Our natural body 'clock' gets thrown into confusion and the result is jet lag.

Every long-distance traveller has his or her own recommendations for overcoming jet lag; there are even elaborate diets you can embark on before you travel to combat its effects. However there is always the theory that concentrating too much on the problem only draws attention to it and almost guarantees you will suffer! For most healthy women, jet lag is *not* a major problem and it is far better not to make too much of an issue of it. Whether or not you succumb depends on a number of factors, including:

How tired you were before you made the journey.

Whether you were fit and well when you set out, or have recently recovered from an illness, are just slightly off-colour, or having your period.

What you eat and drink en route (this is discussed more fully later in this section).

Whether you are flying West or East, or on a North-South route.

This latter point has been the subject of much research, the findings of which seem to be consistent; your bodily rhythms are more upset by flying to the East than to the West — although prevailing winds make a West-East trip shorter, it will normally take you 50 per cent longer to adapt. For example, after a transatlantic flight, your circadian rhythm (from the latin *circa* 'about' and *dies* 'day' — your body's 24-hour pattern of behaviour) will be upset for approximately four days flying West and six days flying East. Flying North-South or South-North causes your body the least problem. Of course, you will suffer from natural fatigue following a long flight, but it does seem that it is crossing the time zones which causes our bodies' disorientation.

Here are some tried and tested suggestions to help avoid jet lag:

Time your arrival   Plan to arrive at your destination as close as possible to your normal bedtime. If you are gaining time, you can, by staying awake a couple of hours later than you normally would, go to bed at a reasonable hour for the country in which you've arrived. Don't try to stay awake until your usual bedtime according to the time at your destination — your body is likely to wake you up again at its normal time, so you will end up having very little sleep and feeling exhausted. If you are losing time, go straight to bed on arrival, the equivalent of having a very late night in your host country's terms. Then, unless you are feeling exceptionally tired or not particularly well, set the alarm to wake you after five or six hours, at what will be mid-morning at your destination. After one, or at most two, further nights, you should have adapted to the new pattern.

If you have difficulty sleeping, or are waking continually during the night, you could try taking a mild sleeping tablet until you adjust. Lack of sleep can be mentally and physically undermining and it would be better to take something to help you sleep for a couple of nights rather than risk fatigue-induced illness spoiling your trip.

Avoid overnight flights when flying East   This causes a short night and so exacerbates the problem of fatigue. I had occasion to test this out recently on a flight from Washington DC to London, the first transatlantic night flight I had ever made. Usually it takes me three to four days to return completely to my normal rhythms after a similar flight during the day, but this time it took a good six days before I felt back to normal.

Local time   Adjust your watch to the local time at your destination as soon as you embark on your journey and accept that as the actual time from then on. Check yourself if you start working out what time it would be at home. If your mind accepts this as the time, the body tends to follow suit. Your time of arrival is always given in local time, so you will not have any problems knowing how long you still have to travel.

Avoid drinking any alcohol   This applies both before departure and on board on a plane. Flying exacerbates the dehydrating effect of the alcohol and even a few drinks could mean that you arrive at your destination with a dreadful headache. Don't drink too many cups of tea or coffee either — both of these are diuretics and so will also promote dehydration — but do drink plenty of water and soft drinks to maintain the body's fluids.

TRAVEL AND YOUR HEALTH

Avoid eating too much   Eating does help to relieve the boredom of a long flight, it is true, which is why the airlines insist on serving so many meals, but it is far better to opt for frequent small snacks than one or two large heavy meals.

Give yourself time to rest   This is especially important after a long-haul flight. The flight itself is physically and mentally wearing and your body will need time to recover. If possible, plan to keep the work load on the first day as light as possible.

Tips for air travellers

1. On long-haul flights, dehydration affects your whole body. To combat the drying effects on your skin, take some moisturizer, handcream and eye gel on board with you and apply them at regular intervals.

2. A combination of dryness and tiredness can leave your eyes feeling sore, so it is an idea to take eyedrops with you too. If you wear contact lenses, make sure your lens case and solution are in your hand luggage, together with a pair of glasses in case you find your eyes need a rest.

3. If you choose an aisle seat rather than one by the window you can stretch your legs and walk up and down in the aircraft when you feel the need. This helps to reduce any swelling in your ankles and reduces the risk of cramps or other muscular aches and pains.

4. Always dress for comfort and wear clothes which can be layered to cope with varying temperatures. Avoid wearing one-piece outfits — they are fine until you need to negotiate the tiny aircraft toilet and then you will require the skills of a latter-day Houdini. Also be careful about what shoes you wear. Always choose fairly loose ones because your feet and ankles will undoubtedly swell up and so tight-fitting shoes can become extremely uncomfortable after a while.

TRAVEL AND YOUR HEALTH

5. If smoking bothers you, check the location of your non-smoking seat carefully. You might find that you have been allocated a seat in the row next to the smoking section, in which case request a different seat. It is also advisable to check the position of your seat in relation to the toilets and the galleys — both these are obviously busy areas and so it is worth avoiding proximity to either of them.

6. Remember to take ear plugs with you — it might be the only way you will get any sleep on the flight.

7. If you have a cold, take a decongestant before you fly, otherwise you may experience increased discomfort from the pressure in your ears.

THE STRESS OF TRAVELLING AND HOW TO MINIMIZE IT

Travelling creates its own brand of tension. Even the excitement you feel about going away on holiday is a form of tension, and business trips can be particularly stressful. Will it go well? Have I made the right preparations? Will I get there on time? These are just a few of the worries that go through your mind before a trip.

There has been much in the press lately about how holidays are actually bad for your health, that the sheer upheaval of going away combined with changes in diet and climate create such high levels of stress that you would have been better off staying at home! If you are one of those women who travel regularly as part of your job, it is crucial to take steps to minimize the risk of such stress if it is not to have a detrimental effect on your health in the long term. So:

• Don't leave everything to the last minute. Start any preparations well in advance to reduce the risk of any panic-making last-minute hitches.

• Don't work until midnight on your last day in the office. Plan your work out so that you have finished everything in time to have a relaxing evening and a good night's sleep.

TRAVEL AND YOUR HEALTH

- Don't travel at the end of a working day — you will invariably end up rushing around, leaving later than you planned, getting caught in heavy traffic on your way to the airport or station and arriving with sweaty palms and pounding heart. You may even end up missing your train/boat/plane entirely, which will do nothing for your blood pressure.

- Don't underestimate how long you need to get to the airport/station/port. It is better to arrive early with time to spare than have to rush.

- Don't plan a meeting for the moment you land. You could be delayed by fog, plane diversions, lost luggage, all sorts of unforseen problems and you will spend the whole journey fretting. Leave yourself a reasonable break between arrival time and your first appointment, preferably long enough to book in to your hotel, unpack, wash and change. Then you can set off to your meeting refreshed and confident.

- Don't drink alcohol for 'Dutch courage' if you are nervous of flying — you will probably only give yourself a fierce headache. If you do feel panic-stricken at the idea of flying, ask your doctor for a mild sedative to help calm you down in the period before you embark.

THE EFFECTS OF TRAVEL ON PERIODS AND PREMENSTRUAL TENSION

You may well find that travelling is disruptive to your normal menstrual cycle, often causing a period to start earlier than you anticipated. For this reason it is wise to be prepared at all times for an unexpected period by carrying tampons or pads with you.

Some women have reported that flying either the day before a period was due or on the day it started greatly increased the amount of pain and cramps they suffered. If you are susceptible to painful periods anyway it would be worth your while to take the dates of your period into account when planning a trip, if you possibly can.

This is equally true if you suffer from that bane of so many women's lives — premenstrual tension. There is no doubt that being in unfamiliar surroundings is going to exaggerate many of the common symptoms of premenstrual tension: a sense of isolation and vulnerability, tearfulness, irrationality, panic attacks. As one sufferer put it, 'If I am away on a trip just before my period starts, I often find myself sobbing uncontrollably about something — I become very depressed indeed sometimes. When I'm at home I certainly get bad tempered, but I rarely get into that sort of state.' Other women have mentioned how 'vulnerable' they feel at this time, especially if everything is not going quite as they had hoped during their trip.

If you do not have to travel too often, you might be able to organize your schedule so that you are not away from home in the few days before a period is due. However if travel is a regular part of your job, this is not always going to be possible and you will need to investigate some of the treatments currently on offer to try and relieve the worst of the symptoms. Dr Michelle Harrison in her book *Self-Help with PMS* (Optima, 1987) outlines five major categories of treatment for premenstrual tension:

1. Lifestyle changes including diet, exercise, stress reduction and relaxation exercises

2. Non-prescription remedies such as vitamins, minerals and food supplements

3. Medicines prescribed by doctors — ie, progesterone, antidepressants, diuretics and others

4. Alternative therapies such as acupuncture and massage

5. Support systems and psychotherapy

Obviously what type of treatment you choose to try depends on your own inclinations and the severity of your symptoms, although the first step with any of them should probably be a consultation with your doctor, to see what advice he or she has to offer on the subject. Much has been written lately about the 'alternative' remedies for PMT and although there is still a lack of truly scientific studies to assess the worth of such treatments, sufficient numbers of women have reported being helped by them to make them worthy of consideration. Quite a few women I have spoken to, for instance, claimed that their symptoms of PMT have been reduced or eliminated by taking supplements of the B vitamins and oil of evening primrose.

If PMT does strike while you are away, try to avoid situations which will only increase the feelings. Don't, for instance, stay shut up in your hotel bedroom. You are much more likely to wallow in misery if you are on your own and out of sight of everyone. Try to go out for a walk, down to the bar for a drink, or just sit in the hotel lounge and read. And avoid the sad novel or the tear-jerking movie on the television, or you might find yourself crying yourself to sleep! One journalist friend who travels a lot

TRAVEL AND YOUR HEALTH

recommends telephoning home when the miseries descend. 'It always helps to hear a familiar and reassuring voice on the other end of the line,' she says, 'I view the call as a kind of treat. I decide I will phone at, say, 10 pm, then I look forward to that and am happy doing other things until the time comes.'

8.
TRAVELLING MOTHERS

Many business women who travel are also mothers; maybe you are currently facing the dilemma of what would happen if *you* had children — would you be able to sustain a career that involved travelling, how would you cope? There are two aspects to this issue, the purely practical one and the emotional one. I have asked several women who have successfully managed to keep on travelling after having children and it was heartening to discover that it is perfectly possible, though not one of them claimed it was as easy as before!

PRACTICAL POINTERS

I was interested to know how soon a woman could expect to resume travelling after having a baby; although there is no hard and fast rule, it depends on how you personally feel about it, a *minimum* emerged of three months after giving birth. If you are breastfeeding and intending to resume travelling, you will need to wean your child on to bottle feeds, starting at least two to three weeks before you intend to go away. Women in this situation recommend expressing milk as early as possible (one suggested starting at the hospital) and giving it by bottle once a day until two weeks before you intend going away, when daytime bottle feeds should commence. Be aware that resuming breastfeeding on your return can be difficult — your baby may reject you, which might increase your feeling of guilt at having gone away in the first place.

From your own point of view, stopping breastfeeding

TRAVELLING MOTHERS

Here mummy... I've done it for you!

abruptly can make you very uncomfortable and could lead to leakages at inconvenient moments; drugs are available to dry up your milk, but I have had reports from a number of women that these drugs have made them feel queasy. Their recommendation therefore is to continue to express milk during your trip.

The practical aspects of leaving children behind when you travel, particularly babies and small children, are, quite obviously, a headache. It is no wonder that women without children regard those who do cope with offspring as a breed of superwomen, as they manage to juggle all aspects of their lives successfully. For most of us, the preparations for the trip itself are quite enough! Needless to say, how easy it is will depend on the level of back-up you have — a helpful partner, granny living nearby, or a good nanny being the ingredients which make it work best. Even if you have all this, don't forget how much *you* are the organizer of events when you are there. You will need to make sure the family will eat when you are away, so fill the freezer and make sure enough money is left for whoever is doing the shopping in your absence, or remind your husband to give the nanny or au pair some funds if she is responsible. Many women told me that they used to indulge in frantic bouts of cooking for the freezer before going away, but no longer do. Fiona was one of these. 'Because I felt guilty about going off and leaving them all alone, I used to spend hours cooking nourishing meals for them to have while I was away. I used to really exhaust myself. Often, I would come back to find the freezer full of these dishes, exactly as I'd left them. They seemed to find it easier to go for convenience foods and takeaways and, quite honestly, I don't think it did them any harm.' In fact, your absence may provide your children with the opportunity to indulge in foods not normally allowed and it will not do them any harm at all. Having a few 'treats', dad bending the rules and providing hamburgers or pizzas, may go a little way to compensating for your absence and will be something they look forward to as an occasional break from routine.

Your children's social life, too, depends on your forward planning. When you are leaving someone else in charge, you will need to leave details of any 'social events' (birthday parties, etc) which will happen in your absence; suggest some activities the children might like to do and leave a float with your nanny or whoever to cover the costs involved. Many travelling mums organize a 'treat' for the children to take place whilst they are away, which will remind them that their mother *does* care, because your going away may make them feel otherwise!

Make sure that whoever is in charge in your absence knows exactly where you are and how to contact you. It is also useful, if your children are at school, to inform the teacher of your travel plans, then should your children exhibit any unusual behaviour in your absence, the teacher will realize the cause for it. Also teachers sometimes like to use your trips as an introduction to some class work about the country or city concerned and this will help your own children feel very positive about your travelling. Indeed, involving your children in what you are doing is very important, so bring back items associated with your trip — currency, model aeroplanes, miniature bags of sugar with unusual designs, match books from hotels and restaurants (remove the matches if they are young), in fact any bits and pieces which could fire a young child's imagination. Children tend to be fascinated with the idea of time differences and love to hear how you were just having your breakfast when they were having their lunch, and so forth. The more you involve them, the less likely they are to resent your going away.

One of the most tiring aspects of travelling when you have children is that you cannot expect to relax when you get home. Children are no respecters of jet lag and will want your attention (and their presents of course!) as soon as you arrive. In order not to disrupt your family's routine entirely, plan to arrive home whilst they are still awake — if you get back late at night they will probably wake up, having been excited about your return, and then you will have difficulty getting them back to bed. Since your homecoming will be anything but restful, plan, if possible, to take an extra day off and arrange for the children to go out with somebody else for part of it, so you can relax. You may find it takes a while for children to get back into their routine when you have been away; they will probably have been allowed to get away with all sorts of things in your absence and may rebel a little at the idea of getting back to normal. Basically, though, children like a routine — it gives them confidence — and they will be quite relieved, deep down, when your reappearance re-establishes it.

Although leaving your children does get easier the older they are, the problems never really go away. Anita, the mother of teenage sons, recounted how she had left one of them at home alone when she went on a business trip. As he was revising for exams, she had decided that money would only tempt him to go out rather than to study, so she had stocked up the freezer and fridge with food for him and left him minimal funds. Unfortunately, the builders who were working in the house turned off the electricity for long enough to turn the carefully prepared food supply into an inedible soggy mess. Her son was forced to scrounge from friends and neighbours until she was able to arrange some money for him!

EMOTIONAL RESPONSES

Psychologically, leaving your children behind is hard to cope with, especially the first few times, although mothers report that it does become easier the more you do it, and the older the children get. One mother described missing her children as a physical thing; the first few separations filled her with a mixture of misery and physical sickness, which stemmed both from guilt at leaving the children behind and panic that something would happen to them. The sheer distance that travel puts between you and your loved ones gives rise to all sorts of morbid thoughts — illness, accidents, abduction by strangers. All the travelling mothers I spoke to agreed that missing one's children was a much more powerful emotion than missing one's husband or lover. However, it only seems to take the experience of a couple of trips where everything went well, everyone coped, nobody came to grief, to enable women to travel without these overwhelming feelings of guilt and unhappiness. Then, travelling alone starts to become a welcome break from the kids, a chance to think about yourself for a change and indulge in a few treats (uninterrupted baths, meals served to *you* for a change). One woman told me she feels she becomes 'someone else' when she travels and can distance herself from her home life and children by taking on a new persona. Another mentioned that the level of missing her children depended very much on what kind of day she had had. If it had gone well, she would feel good about being in 'executive mode', if she felt the day had gone badly, she would tend to feel more 'mumsy' and be very much in need of making a phone call home for reassurance. We all need to feel that we are successful at what we do, so a (temporary) perceived lack of success as an executive is compensated by the feeling that, at motherhood at least, we are doing a good job!

TRAVELLING MOTHERS

Telephone calls home when children are involved can either make you feel terrific or terrible, depending on what you hear — if they sound happy, you are happy too. But do try to get into perspective the tales of the day's disasters recounted to you over the telephone; children are prone to exaggeration, and what they tell you may not be strictly accurate and, most important to remember, they need to blurt it all out to you to make them feel better about it. Try to react calmly and, if you are talking to the child, ask if you can have a word with your husband/nanny/mother and get a more accurate picture of events. Your partner or nanny may also tell you some tale of horror that you wish he or she had kept to themselves until you got home, but don't forget that they probably need the release of talking to you. The important thing is that they *have* coped and you must believe that, having organized the right sort of back-up for your absence, you *can* go off and leave it to other people.

9. DIFFERENT COUNTRIES, DIFFERENT CUSTOMS

When planning a trip abroad it is vital to find out if the country or countries to which you are travelling have any particular customs or business etiquette you should know about. Markets these days cover almost the whole world and you could find yourself in Sydney one day, Tokyo the next and Dubai the day after. Obviously this means you could encounter many widely differing social, political and cultural systems, some of which will be very different from your own, and if you do not have at least a little knowledge of them in advance you could find yourself in some very embarrassing situations.

Trade organizations can advise on the business customs of different countries, or you could approach the commercial section of the relevant embassy or consulate. As well as basic information, such as the office hours and public holidays in that particular country, they can also advise on the details of business protocol and any social customs that should be observed to avoid causing your hosts of clients any offence — things such as, in the Middle East, remembering that the left hand is considered 'unclean' so it is important to accept drinks or food with the right hand. Talking of drink, if you are offered one in the Middle East never ask for a gin and tonic. Most Middle

113

DIFFERENT COUNTRIES, DIFFERENT CUSTOMS

Eastern countries prohibit the drinking of alcohol and any infringements of the rule are met with severe penalties.

In Australia, Britain and the USA it is common practice to use first names fairly soon after initial introductions, but in Japan and Germany addressing a business contact by his or her first name would be deemed most impolite. Japan is a good example of how different business protocol and practices can be from those in, say, Europe and America. For instance, decisions are made by consensus in Japan, and it is important not to press an individual for a decision as this would be considered very rude behaviour. Also there is a strong emphasis on courtesy and politeness, part of which is never openly to disagree with a guest. Consequently a Japanese client may find it difficult to give straightforward answers even in a business context and if he says 'Yes' to something, it does not necessarily mean that he agrees with you, just that he has heard what you are saying. To the Western mentality this can cause considerable confusion and frustration!

Tipping is another social custom that varies dramatically from country to country. We are used to service being built into payments for food and drink and some tipping for other services, such as portering and taxis. In India or Egypt, though, even the slightest service is considered tippable and it is essential to carry a pocketful of loose change expressly for this purpose. In Japan, however, tipping is not a common practice and you could easily cause offence if you are not sensitive to this. These are just a few of the pitfalls that you may encounter on your travels, so be prepared. Find out before you arrive in a country what its customs are.

You might well travel to countries where women do not have the freedom which Western women take for granted. If you travel from Israel to Egypt, for instance, such differences would be highlighted. In Israel a solo business woman would not be unusual and you would be able to travel around with relatively few problems. Egypt, on the other hand, is a country where the majority of the population are Muslim and you may well feel very

DIFFERENT COUNTRIES, DIFFERENT CUSTOMS

uncomfortable as a lone woman anywhere outside the more international business areas. This is not to say that you won't be treated with the greatest care and courtesy by your well-educated business contacts, but you do have to remember that women in Egypt, and all Muslim countries for that matter, hold a very different place in society than do their Western counterparts.

The best way to discover all the little idiosyncrasies of a country is to talk to someone who has been there and so has first-hand experience. For preference, talk to another woman. As already mentioned, women's experiences are very different to men's in a whole host of small but relevant ways and this is particularly true when it comes to doing business. If you are visiting a country where it is unusual for women to hold executive positions, you can find business meetings, which will be almost exclusively with men, awkward and potentially unproductive. Trading on the experience of other women — what has happened, how they coped, how they decided afterwards they *should* have coped — can be enormously helpful in avoiding the pitfalls.

As women ourselves, many of us are naturally very interested in and, indeed, very concerned about, the position of other women in different societies; their treatment often appears unjust to our way of thinking. Many times, you will find yourself wanting to speak out. Remember one thing, you cannot single-handedly change the way things are and it will not do you much good to go on a one-woman revolutionary crusade. In fact, overt and vociferous criticism can be counter-productive. Just by being there in an independent capacity, or as a business person in a country where female executives are rare, sows a few seeds, showing women you meet what is possible and men you meet that dealing with women is not a threat.

If at all possible, talk to local women and find out how *they* feel. Your perception of their situation may be rooted in and coloured by your own cultural values, as Anna discovered when she worked for a period in Greece some years ago. She was disappointed by the lack of women in managerial positions in Greece but when she mentioned this to the many women friends she had made while she was there, she was surprised to find how few of them actually seemed to *want* to do what she had done in terms of independence and career advancement, and that very few felt that opportunities were being kept from them by an essentially male-dominated society. In other words, Anna was transferring the frustrations she would have felt in their position on to them, having arrived at that feeling via a different cultural route. Talking to them gave her a much better understanding of their apparent lack of ambition; she then knew that all she could hope to do was to show them what was possible and let them take it from there.

The subtle contribution to change you can make each time you travel somewhere on your own is more significant than you can possibly realize at the time. Those of us travelling to Japan and the Far East seven or eight years ago remember well being treated as 'honorary men', that appearing to be the only way our male hosts could cope with the strange phenomenon of women holding executive jobs and visiting on business. We were treated wonderfully courteously, but it was a little disconcerting always to work through a, usually male, intermediary-cum-interpreter and to be aware all the time that everyone in the meeting was trying very hard not to look at you!

Over the last few years, much has changed. In Japan in particular, the presence of women in senior positions is much more common than ever before. As one woman who works in an overseas branch of a Japanese bank pointed out, she now has several relatively senior Japanese female colleagues, whereas previously they would have only held clerical positions. And my latest intelligence from the Far East is that our status as 'honorary men' is becoming superfluous, albeit very slowly.

DIFFERENT COUNTRIES, DIFFERENT CUSTOMS

Unless your host raises the subject, avoid getting into political or religious discussions. Even if they do start the ball rolling, it is advisable to tone down your responses if you do not agree with what they are saying. If you are hoping to do business, you will be jeopardizing your chances by entering into arguments on sensitive issues. If the politics of a particular country appal you and you do not feel it is morally justifiable to do business there, you can raise the subject with your company; if they insist on business going on there, maybe someone else could take on that territory instead.

ENTERTAINING

Again how much and what sort of entertaining you undertake on a business trip depends on how senior you are, how well you know your business contacts, the nature of your business — more entertaining goes on in the film world than in the world of banking, for example — and also on the country you are visiting. For instance, in the USA, your hosts will entertain you more as a matter of course than, say, in Sweden.

DIFFERENT COUNTRIES, DIFFERENT CUSTOMS

The etiquette of business entertaining is quite sophisticated. Lunch is most acceptable as a friendly gesture without the implications of a 'bribe' in a business sense or of a desire to become more closely acquainted in a personal one; it is an invitation you can readily accept when travelling on business, particularly as it is often extended to you as a visitor to your host's country. Be a little cautious, however, when issuing offers of lunch yourself. Avoid suggesting lunch to contacts you do not know very well merely because you have a couple of hours to fill. They may interpret it as an attempt to put pressure on them to do business with you. This can be counterproductive.

In America in particular breakfast meetings, often known as the 'power breakfast', have become increasingly popular. Instituted by people who are either incredibly busy or want to appear so — 'Let me see, I think I could fit you in for breakfast Thursday fortnight' — these functions are very useful in the context of a tight schedule on a business trip. They do, in fact, suggest that you are a busy person and that the breakfast will give your guest 'first crack'. They have the advantage of being shorter than lunches, as both of you have got to be somewhere else reasonably early in the day (otherwise, why breakfast?). Many women I know opt for breakfast meetings as they can be less calorific than lunch, preferring a modest, healthy breakfast eaten at the time of day when the body is best equipped to burn up food and with no danger of the temptations of alcohol!

However, be sure to check that meetings at breakfast are accepted practice in the country you are visiting before offering invitations or you might get quite a few raised eyebrows. If you do have breakfast meetings, try to make your hotel the venue. This is a suggestion made entirely for your own benefit as it means you will not risk being late and it will give you extra time to organize yourself for the day. Also allocate plenty of time to breakfast meetings. Your guest could easily arrive late and your discussions may go on longer than you had anticipated, making you late for your next meeting.

Dinner invitations are the most intimate occasions of business entertaining and often provide women with an embarrassing dilemma, especially in countries where the majority of business contacts are men and where it is still unusual for men to come across women in a work context, particularly at a senior level. Many working women travelling alone choose to spend evenings in their hotels rather than issue dinner invitations in the way their male counterparts would not hesitate to do. You may well find yourself in this situation because you fear a dinner invitation might be misconstrued, or have failed to accept one because you suspect it may lead to advances being made that you would really rather not deal with. If you want to invite a client to dinner and feel it might be misinterpreted, suggest that his wife or girlfriend comes too. She may not be able to, or indeed, she may not exist but at least you have established the basis on which the invitation is given.

One of the bonuses about business travel is that some of your business contacts may well become friends, and these are the people you can always entertain without any feeling of pressure or obligation. Why not extend your social contact with them to theatre visits or similar activities? This is not simply self-indulgence, it makes good business sense too. Even if there are no current possibilities for your two companies to do business, they will remember how good you were to deal with in the past and, if any possibility does arise, they will think of you before your competitors.

Entertaining which extends beyond the convention of wining and dining can have wider implications and you should try to judge whether the box at the opera or the day at the races has strings attached, as Jane, a buyer in women's fashion, found out: 'I was delighted to be asked to spend the weekend at a client's country home. They could not have been kinder, even putting a car at my disposal. I had a great time. It so happened that I couldn't place any orders with them after that trip — their range was simply not very exciting for that season. Well, they became quite aggressive and implied I'd been happy enough to accept their generosity and now I wasn't keeping my side of the bargain. I suppose I should have known better, but I just thought they were being kind.' At a certain level, 'treats' outside of work hours are simply 'sweeteners'; only accept them, or only offer them, if your business relationship is a sound, on-going one, which allows for fallow periods too, and you are sure it is how business operates in that particular country or you may, unintentionally, cause considerable offence and find yourself in an awkward situation.

Despite the problems and anxieties that might arise from trying to do business in a society very different from your own, the real excitement of travel rests in these very differences, the chance to see and, if only for a short while, to share in ways of life you have not encountered before. For many of the women I spoke to this was one of the chief bonuses of jobs that involved a lot of travelling.

10. COMING HOME

Do not fall into the trap of thinking that a trip ends when you start out on your return journey, or that this final leg of a trip does not require any planning or forethought. Hassles occurring at this stage can sour completely an otherwise successful and enjoyable time away. Seasoned travellers maintain that it is attention to the simple details that ensure a homecoming is all that is hoped of it and not the anticlimax it is always in danger of becoming if marred by niggly problems. So concentrate on the little things, like:

- Trying to avoid arriving home late at night; not only is travelling at night more hazardous and fraught for a woman alone, but arriving anywhere late at night can make you feel particularly lonely and vulnerable.

- Checking you have sufficient English currency to pay for a taxi or public transport after travelling abroad. Although this seems obvious, it is amazing how easy it is to overlook such a simple detail in the rush and excitement of setting off on the homeward journey.

- Being prepared for delays on the journey home, ie do not make social arrangements for the moment you are due home or everyone could end up feeling let down if you fail to make it because of some hitch en route.

- Making arrangements, if you live alone and have been travelling during the winter months, for a neighbour to come in and put on the heating in the house before you arrive. There is nothing more depressing than walking into a cold, empty house. They might also be persuaded to get in a few supplies for you, such as bread and milk.

COMING HOME

• Phoning home, if you don't live alone, the night before setting off on the homeward journey to confirm arrival times and so on. This prevents any hopes being built up if you have, in fact, had to change your plans for some reason. Children, in particular, need to be sure that you are going to arrive when they are told you will or they can feel let down and resentful and make your homecoming a misery. It also gives those waiting for you at home a chance to set up a welcome committee which is one of the best ways of feeling wanted after a trip!

• Sorting out the mail that has arrived in your absence and putting all the bills and 'threatening looking' mail on one side to be opened the next day when you may feel more able to cope with it. Bills make depressing reading.

• Making sure you have sufficient time to recover if you have been on a long-haul flight or away on a lengthy trip. Do not push yourself too hard — socially or for work — or you will find that fatigue has crept up on you and you will need an even longer time off to recover.

Is is one of the strange facts of travel that when you are away from home it is hard to imagine that life there goes on as normal, which of course it does, and you can quickly get out of the swing of things. One of the main hazards of travelling a lot is that friends lose track of when you are home or away and finally resort to assuming you are always away and forgetting to include you in social events. So it is up to you to re-establish contact with your social circle as soon as you return and have enough energy for social engagements. And make sure you have made time for your husband or lover too.

From a work point of view, analyse quickly the urgent tasks resulting from your trip and get them done immediately. Go through any notes you may have made and expand on them if necessary. It may all seem fresh in your mind at the moment but it is surprising how fast you can forget who said what, which company ordered which product, etc. It also gives you a chance to make an objective assessment of your trip before discussing it with your colleagues. And don't delay in writing to people you have visited to consolidate the impact of your visit.

Before you know it, it will be time to hit the road again! Hopefully what you have read here will make the next time easier and a lot more fun.

INDEX

Africa, 24, 85, 86
AIDS, 76
airlines, 23, 28, 29, 42, 56, 100
airports, 34, 102
alcohol, 96, 99, 102, 114
appointments, 14, 18-21; see also *itinerary, meetings*
Arab countries, see *Middle East*
assertiveness, 54, 55, 58, 63
Australia, 24, 114

babies, see *children*
bathroom, 15, 58
bookings, 9, 16, 18, 55
books, 43, 45, 61, 65, 69; see also *guide books*
breakfast meetings, 118
breastfeeding, 107

Canada, 93
car parking, 15, 16
checking out, 18
checklists, 39, 41-43, 48
children, 75, 107-112, 122
cholera, 86
circadian rhythm, 98
climate, 35, 36, 38
clothing, 34-40, 100
complaining, 56, 57
confidence, see *assertiveness*
couriers, 33
credit cards, 28, 78
currency, 23, 27, 28, 109, 121
customs, 25, 26, 33
cystitis, 34, 92

dehydration, 90, 100
delays, 26, 102, 121
DHSS, 86, 94, 95
diarrhoea, 89, 90
discos, 12
documents, 23-26
drinks, 88, 90, 96, 99; see also *alcohol, water*

driving licence, 24
dry-cleaning, 12

eating, see *food, restaurants*
EEC, 94
Egypt, 114, 115
embassies, 19, 20, 24, 113
entertaining, 117-119
eurocheques, 28
exercise, 15

family, 58, 75, 107, 110; see also *children, partner*
first aid, 92
food, 12, 14, 62, 88, 89, 96, 100, 108; see also *restaurants*
France, 19

Germany, 114
Greece, 94, 115, 116
guide books, 18, 63, 64
guilt, 73, 75, 111

hairdryers, 11, 44
harassment, 39, 40, 60, 61, 68, 79
health, 85-93, 101
Holiday Inns, 12
hospitals, 94
hotel chains, 11, 12, 15
hotel rooms, 13, 15, 54, 56, 58
hotel staff, 11, 56, 57, 72
hotels, 9-14, 62, 71, 102
Hungary, 24
husband, see *partner*

identification, 24
illness, see *health*
immunization, see *vaccination*
India, 25, 40, 90, 114
insects, 87, 88
insurance, 24, 26, 27, 51, 93, 94
international drivers' licence, 25
irons, 44

125

INDEX

Israel, 24, 114
Italy, 61
itinerary, 49, 52, 62, 98; see also
   meetings

Japan, 114, 116
jet lag, 97, 98, 99, 110

loneliness, 58, 60
luggage, 14, 15, 26, 41, 42, 76

malaria, 86, 87
maps, 19, 20, 70
market research, 21, 22
medicines, 41, 91, 93, 103
meetings, 21, 36, 55, 102; see
   also *itinerary*
Middle East, 24, 39, 113, 115
milk, 89, 108, 121
mosquitoes, 87, 88
Muslim countries, see *Middle
   East*

neighbours, 50, 111, 121
noise, 12, 16, 17, 101

office, 48, 49, 101
other guests, 17, 63, 67

packing, 23, 29, 32, 42, 44, 45
partner, 73, 75, 112
passport, 23, 24, 76, 78
periods, 102, 103
plumbing, 16, 51
polio, 86
politics, 117
pregnancy, 94, 97
premenstrual tension, 102-104
public holidays, 19, 113

receipts, 25, 94
relaxation, 15, 60, 97, 100
reservations, see *bookings*
restaurants, 62, 63, 68, 77, 89,
   118; see also *food*
romance, 70, 72, 75, 76
Romania, 24
room service, 12, 63

samples, 32, 33
Saudi Arabia, 24; see also
   Middle East
Scandinavia, 19, 62
schedule, see *itinerary, meetings*
school, 109, 110
secretary, 48, 49
security, 16, 31, 42, 50, 51, 72,
   76
self-protection, 78, 79
sex, see *harassment, romance*
shoes, 35, 36, 44, 45, 61, 100
sightseeing, 14, 60, 61, 65
sleeplessness, 16, 17, 99
smallpox, 87
smoking, 96, 101
South America, 86
stress, 53, 101
suitcases, 29-31
sunburn, 91

taxis, 14
telephone, 52, 105, 112, 122
television, 13, 17, 22, 104
telex, 12
thieves, 26, 51, 77, 78; see also
   security
thrush, 34, 92
tickets, 24, 76
tipping, 114
tourist offices, 18-20
travel agents, 10, 23, 27, 85, 93
travel guides, see *books, guide
   books*
travel sickness, 93, 95, 96
travellers' cheques, 27, 28, 76,
   78
typhoid, 86

USA, 15, 24, 55, 56, 60, 62, 93,
   118
USSR, 24

vaccinations, 85, 86
visas, 23, 24

water, 88; see also *drinks*

yellow fever, 86

ABOUT THE AUTHOR

Roberta Bailey studied French and German at Exeter University and then interpreting at Oxford Polytechnic.

Since 1973 she has been selling rights in British books to publishers all over the world. Her work involves a great deal of travelling, usually on her own, and over the years she has had to face and overcome a number of different problems. This book, her first, is based on her own experience and that of the many other women she has interviewed who travel alone either on business or by choice.

Roberta Bailey is married and lives in London.